THE GASLIT DIARIES

Kylie Cheung

**THOUGHT
CATALOG
Books**

Art direction and design by KJ Parish. Cover by GloriAnne Rose Dairo. Published by Thought Catalog Books, a publishing house owned by The Thought & Expression Company. It was published in 2018.

ISBN 978-1-949759-01-3

FOREWORD

When I'm sometimes asked why I'm so passionate about feminism, I typically offer a response to the tune of "because I read the news." But the truth is, it's a lot more personal than that.

The loved ones and others in my life who have seen the activist work I do, read my writing, and witnessed the backlash I face for all of it have told me I am strong. And sometimes they ask me how I *became* strong.

Experiencing sexual violence when I was a teenager didn't make me "strong." Being harassed and called a whore outside women's health clinics, also when I was a teenager, and needed, not wanted, reproductive health care, didn't make me "strong" either. Like all young women, I have always been strong. But in those moments that I was forced to feel ashamed, embarrassed, and small, I was shown where, from then on, I would choose to direct my strength: to feminism—the social, political, and economic empowerment of marginalized people—so no one else would have to go through what I did.

I am strong because I am a woman, because I face what all women face every day simply for *being* women. And I am a feminist because the personal is the political.

I wrote this book in the summer of 2018 and edited it in the fall. I wrote this foreword on the day that Brett Kavanaugh, a wealthy, powerful white man accused of sexual assault and misconduct by multiple women, was confirmed to the Supreme Court. I wrote this because what's happening today breaks my heart. But here is what I know—from my own experiences, and also, yes, from reading the news: It's not over.

When Clarence Thomas, credibly accused of groping and harassing multiple women, was confirmed to the Supreme Court, we—women, survivors, allies—didn't give up and go home. When Donald Trump, accused of sexual abuse by more than 20 women, was elected president, we didn't give up and go home. All the times this president and his cabinet, through rhetoric and policies, have laughed in the faces of women and survivors, we didn't give up and go home. And you can bet your life an entitled man-child named "Brett" is not going to be what sends us packing.

No single outcome will ever end this fight. Brett Kavanaugh's confirmation, like the election of Donald Trump over Hillary Clinton two years earlier, is just one part of the fight of our lives, for our lives: to be respected, to be seen, to be *believed*.

As women, we are not collateral damage for your political agendas. Our freedom, safety, and livelihoods are nonexpendable, nonnegotiable. Our bodies are not state incubators.

In voting to confirm Kavanaugh, U.S. senators told women and survivors that they do not think we matter, that affirming male hegemony, dismantling women's most fundamental freedoms, and telling men it is their birthright to treat women however they want without consequences, are all of higher priority than our rights, our dignity, our existence.

Republican senators and the president stood by Kavanaugh,

insisting that it must be him and no other, not despite but *because* of the message his confirmation sent to women and survivors: that this is not our country, that, for all the progress made by the recent #MeToo movement to address systemic sexual abuse, men still rule. The president and nearly every leading Republican senator who facilitated Kavanaugh's confirmation owe their careers to patriarchal forces and brutish, relentless misogyny, to political platforms that guaranteed the debasement of American women en masse. Misogyny and cruelty are not mere accidental facets of the Republican Party or the Trump presidency; rather, they are the foundations of both.

These have not been easy times to be a woman, but I am so grateful to have had the opportunity these past few years to see who is good, to work and connect with the most incredible people, and to find the courage to say and do things I never imagined I would be able to before November 2016.

Believe women. Believe survivors. To all women and allies—stand up for what you believe is right and stand up to what you know is wrong. But whatever you do, don't look away. Don't be silent. What's happening in this country today is wrong. You know it, I know it, and we must all stand arm-in-arm and refuse to accept it.

CONTENTS

THE GASLIT WORLD

For me, apology comes as reflex. I'm an adult woman who still stammers "sorry" to a chair at least once or twice a week, and as embarrassing as this reality is, I know I'm not alone. Women are born and raised to feel sorry for taking up space; we apologize for being bumped into while walking down busy streets, we apologize for being interrupted when speaking, we apologize for almost being hit by cars when the walk sign is on. And, of course, I realize the irony of this. Men can't apologize for committing sexual violence—nor, often, even acknowledge sexual violence as a problem in society—while women can't stop apologizing, for, well, everything.

I wish I could say that I've retired this habit since becoming a feminist. But as the saying goes, old habits die hard—and so, too, does internalized misogyny. That said, I'll never forget the first, real time I chose not to say sorry.

I was 16 and willfully selfish; I didn't care or think about much beyond grades and clothes and having a good time. My disinclination toward bras and embrace of casual relationships had almost nothing to do with feminist rebellion, and everything to do with the characteristic brazenness of a teenager who just didn't care. (Which, I guess, in itself is arguably feminist; I assigned value to my comfort and happiness—something that's really only gotten harder to do as I've grown older.)

It should go without saying that the experience of sexual harassment was nearly routine for me at that stage of my life. I tried to elevate myself above consciousness of what people said, and I often did. My life, again, really boiled down to three things when I was 16: grades, clothes, having fun. And yet, every now and then I would fantasize about reporting harassment I experienced, making a beeline to the principal's office and repeating every unsavory, gendered word I often heard attached to my name—slut, whore, the works. But for a long stretch of time, I never did.

After all, how was I supposed to prove it, any of it?

That question—how I could "prove it"—preemptively stopped me from talking about a lot of things I'd experienced growing up, for a long, long time; and it often still restrains me, even today. It shuts down occasional thoughts of blurry sexual encounters that left me feeling hurt and confused, of backhanded, sexist comments and acts which I could never quite prove were made out of ill-will and deliberate misogyny.

In either case, when I finally had proof and only when I had proof of the harassment I'd experienced, I made the trek to my vice principal's office, and revealed a barrage of receipts: texts from a classmate calling me a whore and slut for sharing fully clothed but bra-less photos of myself on social media, for my sexual decisions, for taking birth control, and so on, and so forth.

I didn't expect the process or what happened next to be easy, but I certainly didn't expect it to be so frustrating. (Naive, I know, but I was 16.)

I had gone to her office because I refused to be shamed, to feel sorry for my fashion choices or private decisions I made about my body. To all the bicyclists that had almost run me down and all the boys in my classes who would cut me off mid-sentence, I had apologized each and every single day. But I refused to apologize for this.

When I entered her office and proceeded to "prove it," I was briefly questioned about what I had said or done to instigate the harassment and what I had been wearing in the pictures in question, and other questions along those lines, before my complaints seemed to be dismissed altogether. This was a few years ago, so I can't quite quote her verbatim, but it went something like this: "He's a 17-year-old boy. They make mistakes, you know how it is. Once he receives a warning, I'm certain it won't happen again. I'll talk to him, then we can all sit down, you can both exchange apologies."

All I really remember from that dialogue was standing frozen with embarrassment and confusion. I'd never made myself more vulnerable to someone who was frankly a stranger to me, and reluctantly opened up about private matters of my life that in no way justified a classmate calling me a whore—only to be partially blamed for the harassment I'd experienced, and all while a 17-year-old boy was almost wholly absolved of any responsibility whatsoever for anything he'd said to me.

I will say that consequences were doled out eventually, but only after my imposing, self-assured parents walked me into the office the next morning armed with a student conduct code that explicitly listed suspension as the punishment for sexual harassment. My voice as a young woman alone certainly hadn't been enough.

You don't have to tell me how common of an experience

this is—sexual harassment, misogynist bullying, young men facing zero accountability, victim-blaming. I know. I certainly don't pretend to bring new experiences or particularly new ideas to the table in writing this; women have been shouting their experiences and ideas for years, only to be dismissed and ignored. In telling this story, I acknowledge all of those experiences and ideas, and the relative lack of originality of what I'm writing. But I share my story nonetheless because I've seen enough mediocre, unoriginal male ideas given the time of day to know that what I have to say as a young woman is good and important enough to share.

In either case, what always stuck with me about this particular incident from my high school years was my vice principal's suggestion that this was somehow normal, as well as her casual assumption that I, too, would just accept this as normal. *They make mistakes, you know how it is.* Making the conscious decision to call a young woman a slut is not a "mistake." It's an abusive act, and it's not normal. And sure, maybe sexual harassment *is* "normal" to the extent that it's an unfortunate reality that women and girls face every day. But it *shouldn't* be normal. We shouldn't accept or expect others to just accept it.

That was the first time I remember feeling gaslit—manipulated into questioning whether what I knew wasn't normal actually was. And that feeling has stuck with me since that day in 2015. I've spent every day, since, listening and watching and knowing in my heart that so much of what's happening around me and in this country isn't right, isn't normal.

But what *is* normal, for young women and feminists, at least, is gaslighting. With every "calm down," "it's not that bad," "well, actually," and "well, that's normal" that's directed at us, we're told that our own recollection of our experiences with oppression is wrong, that our concept of reality is wrong, that our grip on it is tenuous. Women and girls live in a gaslit world that tells us—typically using cynical boys and men as its mouthpiece—that harassment and abuse are just "free speech"; that issues as fundamental and existential as abortion rights are things we should all, as Ohio Gov. John Kasich once so eloquently put it, just "chill" about; that men are paid more than women because girls are afraid of math and science; that women who accuse men of sexual abuse have become the real predators.

Our pain, our experiences, our trauma, and our reality are so often boiled down to two words—"prove it"—as if to say, if a man can't wrap his head around what you, a woman, face every day, then it must not be real. If you can't convince him, then it isn't real. Because if a man determines that it is not real, therefore, it is not.

We, women, are fundamentally lacking in credibility. And, of course, that's because the fact remains that much of America still hates women. The evidence of this is sound, although shockingly enough, most men have chosen to ignore it.

As author Cheryl Strayed put it in her 2017 essay, "Someday, a 'Nasty' Woman Like Hillary Clinton Will Win," the 2016 presidential election was itself a "referendum on how much America still hates women." Yet, in the absence of any legitimate explanations for Clinton's electoral college loss other than racism, loathing of diversity, and, of course, misogyny, all sorts of faux-intellectual, identity-neutral guesses have been thrown around to explain her loss in a more roundabout manner, rather than concede that many Americans are actually bigots. These roundabout explanations were meant to allow us to avoid tough conversations about reality: that many parts of our country, if not our country at large, remain steeped in crass, relentless misogyny. And even as we all watched said crass, relentless misogyny unfold on television screens across the country on the night of Nov. 8, 2016, we were subsequently told that it wasn't that, that making things about gender and identity had been precisely why we'd lost. Each and every one of these explanations comprised a master class in gaslighting.

In an ideal world, my words and observations would be enough. I would speak of these things that have happened in my life—that happen every day in my life and so many other young women's lives—and you would believe me, and we could move on. But if the events of the past few years have revealed anything, it's that this is not an ideal world at all. It's a gaslit world. And that's why I've put together this book.

BACK WHEN THE UNITED STATES was just a little bit younger, "free speech" meant something else entirely. It meant young people marching in the streets to protest wars, journalists speaking truth to power, and everyone freely believing in whatever religion they chose to believe in. Don't get me wrong—this country's history is paved with gross inequalities in terms of how the First Amendment's promise has been delivered. Racial inequalities, sexual inequalities, and, of course, gendered inequalities. And yet, when someone said the words free speech, or the First Amendment, that was what we envisioned as the ideal: peaceful protests, diligent reporters, people of all faiths being able to practice their religion without facing racist travel bans and being subjected to hate crimes.

For many of us, this still is the ideal. But it's no longer what comes to mind when we hear the words "free speech."

Now, those words are associated with the likes of Richard

Spencer, Milo Yiannopoulos, Ben Shapiro, and a number of other well-known, right-wing "provocateurs," culminating a pathetic push to portray unapologetic racists, misogynists, and xenophobes as martyrs of ideological intolerance. Think about it. Whenever Spencer or Yiannopoulos are protested or turned away from a university they attempt to speak at, often due to valid safety concerns, the internet is all at once drowned in op-eds about how college students and the "intolerant left" are somehow violating the First Amendment rights of white supremacists.

But the First Amendment is not the right to a platform and audience, any and everywhere, on demand; for example, the White House wouldn't be violating your free speech rights if it declined to let you broadcast yourself from its Facebook Live feed. Not being given a platform is not the same thing as censorship.

The First Amendment isn't just a flag to wave when you want to say something terrible and force others to listen, nor is it a shield to defend yourself from the social or professional consequences of your words and actions. Much of what the First Amendment's most vocal right-wing advocates claim it protects or necessitates, in reality, it does not.

I'm not going to get into the nitty-gritty of how (justified) outrage and receiving any attention whatsoever grants far-right activists the only power they have. It just seemed worth pausing to explain why white supremacists should not be the modern faces of the free speech movement in this country, nor should they be regarded as victims just because most decent, sensible people don't want to listen to them spew hate.

In either case, the reality is that ever since the 2016 election, those with violently hateful ideologies of bigotry directed at people across lines of gender, orientation, race, and citizenship status, have become emboldened—in their speech, in their political participation, and, at the expense of marginalized people's safety, in their actions. And the speech of bigots, given a platform, is indisputably harmful to this nation's most vulnerable people—and their ability to engage in free speech.

In nine U.S. metropolitan areas, hate crimes in the United States rose by almost 25 percent between 2015 and 2016, targeting people of color, immigrants, and Muslim people, according to research published by the Center for the Study of Hate and Extremism. All of the affected groups had been targeted by inflammatory rhetoric and discriminatory policy proposals pitched by then-candidate Donald Trump, who announced his candidacy for president in June 2015 with a speech that sweepingly identified Mexican immigrants as criminals and rapists. (Trump, for his own part, has been accused of sexual misconduct by roughly two dozen women as of 2018, and boasted about sexually assaulting women on leaked audio from 2004.)

Since being elected, President Trump has only doubled down on attacking marginalized groups, with policies that have included separating migrant families fleeing rape and domestic violence, and locking migrant babies and children in literal cages. He's equated migrants and people of color to animals and vermin, fought tooth-and-nail for a travel ban on Muslim-majority countries, and his administration has claimed accusations of sexual assault should only be taken seriously when the accused man has confessed to wrongdoing. Frankly, the list of dangerously intolerant comments the president has made could go on forever; after all, this is a man who has said some neo-Nazis are "very fine people," in reference to white supremacist protesters who assaulted counter-protesters and even killed one person at a rally in Charlottesville in 2017.

You get the point. Trump's words are not only normalizing hatred and turning marginalized people into targets, but as the uptick in hate crimes and racist violence indicates, they're also inseparable from the identity-based threats, violence, and harassment that have increased in the United States ever since he rose to political prominence.

In 2018, an unprecedented number of self-avowed white nationalists ran for office across the country, up and down the ballot, and some were met with disturbing levels of success, according to Southern Poverty Law Center's tracking. One self-identified white nationalist candidate won a special election as part of the Republican Party in Washington state. Another, who spoke openly about having raped his wife and vocally advocated for incestuous relationships between father and daughter, ran for Congress in Virginia after a previous attempt garnered a small percentage of the statewide vote.

Meanwhile, around roughly the same time candidate-Trump suggested there should be "some form of punishment" for women who have abortions, and sweepingly equated all abortions to the act of "ripping" out a nine-month "baby" at a presidential debate, a report by the Feminist Majority Foundation revealed that in 2015, three abortion providers in the U.S. were murdered, and nine were subjected to attempted murders. The following year, 34.2 percent of U.S. abortion providers surveyed reported receiving "severe violence or threats of violence" in the first half of 2016 alone, compared with the previous high of 24 percent throughout 1995.

Speech is never really just speech. White supremacists complain of oppression, such as social ostracism and censorship, directed at them, without taking any responsibility for the real-life devastation and violence that extends as a direct result of their words. Truly, it requires a lifetime of privilege and an inflated sense of entitlement for one to equate free speech to consequence-free speech. Which makes sense, considering a lifetime of privilege and inflated sense of entitlement are often the defining characteristics of people who grow up in a world that is structured around their experience as the default.

And all of this relates to young women and feminists, too. Specifically, there's a shockingly prevalent free speech issue that we often waste far too much time bickering about Milo Yiannopoulos to even acknowledge: Young women and girls are being forced to censor themselves—on the internet, and everywhere—to dodge harassment, stalking and doxxing. Since identity-based harassment always targets people on an intersectional level, girls and women of color and LGBTQ people often face the brunt of it. And the misogynist, racist, and generally intolerant speech they are subjected to has real, lived consequences: namely, the silencing of young women.

Half of all girls in the United Kingdom report having experienced harassment on the internet, according to a 2017 survey by the children's charity Plan International UK. A 2013 study by the International Women's Media Foundation revealed 46 percent of women journalists have reported experiencing sexual harassment, including rape threats, while doing their job; in 2017, Vox shared a feature telling the stories of female journalists who left their industries after being overwhelmed by the gendered harassment they faced. And according to a 2018 survey by the National Network to End Domestic Violence, 50 percent of women respondents who reported being harassed online said they received direct, violent threats to them or people they knew.

The threats of rape and instances of sexual abuse on the internet, a platform that enables users to hide behind a mask of anonymity and face virtually zero accountability, are unquantifiable. And if you don't feel like taking my word for it, feel free to ask nearly any other young woman who regularly uses the internet—especially those who express opinions supporting feminist and social justice issues on their social media channels.

What's also unquantifiable is how many girls and women are forced to self-censor just to protect themselves from the aforementioned abuses. Right-leaning "free speech" proponents uphold the marketplace of ideas as sacred, but utterly disregard the power dynamics inherent to this philosophy. How can women, people of color, LGBTQ people and other marginalized groups who face harassment, threats, and violence for no reason other than who they are, contribute to this marketplace on an equal level with their white, male counterparts, in these circumstances?

Sure, white supremacists and far-right bloggers face plenty of backlash on the internet when they express their bigoted views. But to conflate these experiences with those of young women and feminists is a gross false equivalence. White supremacists and misogynists are shunned and ostracized on college campuses and other spaces, not because of any aspect of their identity, but because of their active, conscious decision to advocate for marginalized groups to be harassed, attacked and denied basic rights. And further, it's difficult if not impossible to defend their ideologies and political speech as nonviolent, when there exists an inherent violence in ideologies that involve stripping whole groups of people of their rights against their will.

Those who engage in such hate speech may lose their jobs

or face social ostracism and other similar consequences. But how can this treatment be unjust when it is a direct response to people's actions and decisions, as opposed to immutable aspects of their identity? Being fired from your job for threatening to rape young women on social media is quite different from being subjected to rape threats and harassment as punishment for having the audacity to be a girl and use the internet.

We should devote far more of our discussions of free speech to considering the plights of those who have unequal opportunities to engage in speech—people of color, women and girls, LGBTQ people, low-income people struggling to access WiFi, and so on and so forth. Our conversations about whose free speech is being limited should not revolve around white supremacists.

Hate speech and the violence it often yields may be "free speech." But in the same vein, to simplify and reduce violent rhetoric and threats to mere "free speech" is gaslighting, plain and simple, and doing so serves to erase the deeply harmful consequences of hate speech.

Don't allow anyone to convince you that what we're seeing—the hate crimes, the mass online harassment, the record-breaking numbers of white supremacists running for public office without shame—is just free speech at work, that all free speech is one and the same, that any of this is somehow normal.

These days, the truth is so often obfuscated by internet hot takes, void of meaningful context about the disparities in lived experience across different groups of people. So let's just be clear: What we're seeing—and specifically, what we're hearing—is not normal. And anyone who's spent more time listening to girls and women and people of color who are routinely harassed on the internet, and less time reading editorial columns about the "persecution" of conservative college students, could tell you that.

———————————————

OF COURSE, GASLIGHTING TAKES FORM not only when young women are told that something terrible and wrong is "normal," but also when they're told that something terrible, wrong and pervasive isn't "that bad."

I don't pretend to be an expert about the modern landscape of reproductive rights in this country—it's complicated, nuanced, and varies widely across regions. Far too many people—mostly men, religious figures, talk show hosts, and politicians—pretend to be experts, and I'm not here to play along with their charade. But I have had the tremendous privilege of working with women who *are* experts, women who have had abortions, and women whose careers are quite literally to help others have abortions and access other crucial reproductive health care. I've had the privilege of covering the issue on a regular basis as a writer, and have even written a weekly column recapping the news in reproductive rights for the past couple years at The Mary Sue. Reproductive rights are an issue that I'm deeply passionate about, write about regularly, and make a real, concerted effort to keep up with.

And I know I'm not alone in this. As a voting bloc, young women care deeply about women's rights and being represented by women political leaders they know they can count on to be their advocates. Polling from 2018, the first major election year after Donald Trump was elected president, revealed a third of young women (age 18 to 34) would prefer to vote for a female candidate over a male one, and 65 percent of young women believe the country would change for the better with more female leaders, all while women across the country ran for office and won their races in unprecedented numbers. Between 2016 and 2018, the number of women running for Congress increased by 60 percent.

Young women volunteer. They vote. And yes, they care. Now, whether or not patriarchal society feels inclined to validate and respect that caring is a separate story entirely.

In 2017, toward the end of my freshman year of college, Democratic Party leadership started to become more vocal in defending and supporting anti-abortion Democrats. Unsurprising in light of his approach to "identity politics"—that is, castigating or outright ignoring these issues—Vermont Sen. Bernie Sanders even endorsed an anti-choice mayoral candidate in Nebraska.

And it wasn't just Sanders. That same year, Democratic National Committee chair Tom Perez called on Democrats to embrace a "big tent" party, including Democrats who would vote against women's rights. And a bit later that year, Democratic Congressional Committee (DCC) chair and New Mexico Rep. Ben Lujan declared the DCC would support and fundraise for anti-choice Democratic candidates.

The underlying message of their claims was that advocacy for women's bodily autonomy and equal status—which abortion is inherently, inextricably tied to—are disposable for perceived political advantage, and refusal to compromise on whether women are entitled to human rights is a sort of toxic intolerance.

I was annoyed, afraid, angry, and insulted by this trend; so were many women, feminists, and allies. In that political moment, abortion rights felt like an almost existential point of conflict within this Party—how could our leadership financially patronize, encourage and support candidates who would use their power to support the government's ability to force women to give birth? How could they use us—women, and our human rights—as bargaining chips, and reduce us to collateral damage for hypothetical electoral victories? It felt like a betrayal; rather than simply put in the work to mobilize and draw larger voter turnout in red states, instead, our leaders had opted to throw us under the bus. And for the record, more than a year later, this issue hasn't quite gone away for the Party. Until more women—especially women who have had abortions—have a seat at the table, it never will.

Around the same time all of that was happening, I remember discussing the issue with a then-recent ex over coffee. When I'd finished speaking—between numerous interruptions, of course—he looked confused.

"I don't understand what the big deal is."

The "big deal" is that women's fundamental human rights aren't something that can just be compromised on, I said.

"But I don't see how this could split the Party. Most of the electorate, most voters, really don't care about abortion. It's just a women's issue."

Report after report had shown how evangelical loathing of women's rights had given Trump a crucial, narrow boost in the 2016 election. And, of course, *women* care about abortion rights; there are dozens of women-led groups that exist solely to fight for this cause. And yet, nothing I said really seemed to convince him.

Maybe he was right about something. When it comes to abortion rights, it's not just a matter of being "pro-life" or pro-choice: There's also rabid, insidious apathy. Plenty of people don't care about whether women have abortions or not—but they also don't care about whether or not women are able to access abortion.

In July 2018, Supreme Court Justice Anthony Kennedy announced his retirement, spelling the likelihood *Roe v. Wade*, the landmark decision that made abortion legal on the federal level, would either be overturned or thoroughly gutted in the next few years.

His retirement endangered a number of human rights, considering the radically intolerant ideologies of the president who would choose his successor. But abortion rights were indisputably on the table, and even as the consequences of this would be life-or-death for women, far too few people—even liberal-leaning people who felt strongly about immigration, voting rights, and police brutality—seemed to really care.

Fifty-four and 53 percent of respondents to one national poll, at the time, said it was "very important that the next Supreme Court justice share their views on immigration and voting rights," respectively, while just 47 percent said the same about abortion rights. So, maybe he was right. Maybe there are, in fact, many people who don't care about abortion.

Like all issues that disproportionately affect women, reproductive rights are relegated to "women's issue" status—irrelevant and unimportant to the mainstream, or, as my ex put it, to "most people." The term "women's issues" arises from the universal understanding that men and the male experience are the default.

The truth is that we're all affected by reproductive rights because reproductive rights affect the extent to which every single born, living person is able to autonomously participate in society and contribute to the economy. The framing of reproductive rights as merely a "women's issue"—and the framing of women's issues, in general, as somehow inherently less consequential—is just more gaslighting. It's a reductive narrative that is meant to trick women into believing our experience is not part of the mainstream, despite how we comprise more than 50 percent of the U.S. population.

In either case, our chat over coffee eventually shifted to a new topic. You can't teach empathy, you can't magically string the right words together to instill it in someone who is fundamentally lacking. So I didn't try. But before we moved on, he added, "And abortion is legal. There's nothing left to fight about."

It's been more than a year since that conversation, and over the course of that year, I've heard repeated iterations of that particular argument at different points in the news cycle.

One has really stuck with me. In an interview with *New York Magazine*, Ohio Gov. John Kasich, the same man who signed a 20-week ban on abortion into law in his state, responded to a question about abortion by insisting that we all just "take a chill pill." Kasich, who identifies as "pro-life," said his wife was pro-choice, and "we don't sit around arguing about this."

Well, great, just great. Good for them. But let's get a couple things straight, the first being that this is gaslighting.

If there's one thing women—and anyone who cares about our health, living standards and rights—should feel about abortion rights today, it's a sense of urgency and outrage.

Around 27 percent—that's more than a quarter—of all of the roughly 1,200 restrictions on abortion enacted since *Roe v. Wade* (1973) were passed in the five short years between 2011 and 2016. As of 2014, around 90 percent of all counties in the U.S. do not have an abortion provider; in 2017, the Population Reference Bureau released a study that revealed millennial women's living standards are worse than their mothers' due to the sharp decline in access to women's health centers over the last decade.

The United States has the highest maternal mortality rate in the industrialized world at 26.4 deaths per 100,000 live births, and it's not even close. The maternal mortality rate is even higher—and substantially so—in states with more restrictions on access to abortion, and for women of color.

Pretending that women are exaggerating the crisis we currently face or the extent to which our ability to end a pregnancy affects every aspect of our lives and economic circumstances is gaslighting. Full stop. And so, too, is pretending that this is an issue we can all just gather around, hold hands, and agree to disagree about. The suggestion that compromise on abortion rights is even possible ignores the vastly disproportionate power dynamics in play: Lawmakers who "agree to disagree" with the women they're supposed to serve are ultimately still the ones who make the final decision about the laws governing those women's bodies.

For some perspective, our Congress, which routinely attempts to defund Planned Parenthood and ban abortion at varying stages, is 80 percent male as of 2018. State legislatures across the country, which routinely pass bans and restrictions on abortion rights that disproportionately target low-income women, women of color, LGBTQ people, and women in rural areas, are 75 percent male.

And the vast, overwhelming majority of the lawmakers in these state legislatures who introduce restrictions on abortion are white Republican men. In January 2017, 71 percent of all anti-abortion legislation introduced across the country were proposed by white Republican men, and 25 percent by white Republican women. The majority of women who have abortions, or face greater barriers to access abortion care, are women of color, and opposition to abortion by some women doesn't somehow make restrictions "woman-approved," or negate the harm these restrictions inflict on many women's lives.

Here is the reality that the Kasichs and my ex-boyfriends of the world are either willfully ignorant to or cruelly gas-lighting us about: The ability to access abortion can be life-or-death, and affects every aspect of women's lives. Even if every single woman had access to reliable birth control, free and on demand, it's worth noting the majority of abortions involve pregnancies that were conceived while using contraception.

In other words, abortion rights still solely boil down to whether the government can force women to give birth, and in doing so, reduce us to second-class citizens. And you'll have to forgive me if I'm not inclined to "agree to disagree" about whether women's ambitions, aspirations, and overall liveli-hood are of less value than the hypothetical of a child.

(MANY) MEN WANT FEMINISTS to calm down and ac-cept that we are now living in a post-gender world—a world where abortion is a settled non-issue, and a world where every perceived inequality, every single inconvenience women face but men do not, is the fault of the individual and only the individual. Which is the perfect segue into my next topic of discussion: the gender wage gap.

In 2016, Ohio State University published a study that re-vealed women working in STEM still earn 31 percent less than men working in STEM. In other words, the wage gap has nothing to do with women loathing science, and every-thing to do with sexism and discrimination, plain and simple.

Of course, this 31-point gap dropped to 11 percent when accounting for how "women tended to graduate with degrees in fields that generally pay less than fields in which men got their degrees," the study showed. The gender wage gap across the board, including non-STEM fields, sits at roughly this same number—11 percent—when all factors such as field, education level, and experience are weighed.

Ask the men in your life why this is, and you're likely to hear some variation of how the gap only exists because women actively choose to avoid higher paying work. I know I've certainly heard this before, over and over, and either my experience is just a frustrating outlier, or a lot of men just blame women for the fact that women are paid less than men, and are far more likely than men to live in poverty or be housing insecure.

But the wage gap starts somewhere, and that somewhere is a culture that pushes women away from higher-paying fields from the get-go. Growing up, girls are substantially less likely to have role models working in STEM or other high-paying lines of work, with whom they can directly relate.

In 2016, *The New York Times* published an article called, "As Women Take Over a Male-Dominated Field, the Pay Drops," which examined a study by researchers at Cornell University which revealed that when women enter a field in greater numbers, pay decreases. In other words, the feminization of industries, due to the perception that if women are doing it, then the job is therefore easier and less valuable, ranks among the ultimate contributors to the wage gap.

A key excerpt from the *Times* article:

> "Consider the discrepancies in jobs requiring similar education and responsibility, or similar skills, but divided by gender. The median earnings of information technology managers (mostly men) are 27 percent

higher than human resources managers (mostly women), according to Bureau of Labor Statistics data. At the other end of the wage spectrum, janitors (usually men) earn 22 percent more than maids and house-cleaners (usually women).

"Once women start doing a job, 'It just doesn't look like it's as important to the bottom line or requires as much skill,' said Paula England, a sociology professor at New York University. 'Gender bias sneaks into those decisions.'"

Majors like English, women's studies, anthropology, history, and the humanities in general easily lead to meaningful, impactful work. Our disrespect for and stereotyping of these disciplines as easy and lazy, just because they're often female-dominated or lead to female-dominated lines of work, is inherently gendered.

Another important study has revealed the role of paid maternal leave instead of paid family leave in contributing to gendered pay disparities. A 2015 study by Cornell found paid maternity leave laws resulted in women being 5 percent more likely to remain employed, but 8 percent less likely to be promoted or hired. This is the obvious result of stereotyping all women as likely to become mothers, and the gendered notion that having children will cause seismic shifts affecting female employees' abilities to work, but fail to cause so much as a ripple in male employees' worlds.

Child-rearing should affect men and women's lives equally, and therefore, impact their working situations and pay prospects equally. But that's not the case.

Women are not being paid less because of their individual

choices, but due to archaic attitudes about American families, and the systemic devaluation of women's work and skills.

Additionally, all women can attest to how gender shapes whether you're taken seriously, or viewed as authoritative, senior, and deserving of a promotion or raise. In 2016, an Australian study revealed women negotiate for raises at equal rates as their male colleagues, but are 25 percent less likely to receive these raises upon negotiation. And there isn't a statistic in the world that could account for how discrimination and subliminal sexism impact every aspect of how women are treated in the workplace, from being shut out of boys' club meetings, to seeing their ideas ignored and then co-opted and re-shared by their male peers. The loss of women's opportunities on the basis of gender is frankly unquantifiable.

Even the staunchest of male allies could never fully comprehend what it's like to be perceived as weak, unauthoritative, and unworthy for reasons that are entirely out of our power to change. When it comes to discussing the wage gap with men, you'd be hard-pressed to find one who didn't demand "proof." Sure, maybe not all men demand this. But mainstream narratives around the wage gap are generally focused on blaming women—either for our choice in career path, or for failing to be proactive and negotiate—and gaslighting us into accepting that anything wrong in our lives is due to our own actions, and not the all-encompassing sexism to which we are subjected.

These narratives are rooted in society's failure to believe women and accept our words and accounts of our experiences at face value. That's why nearly every point women make about our everyday experiences is met with cynicism and the words "prove it." The wage gap is no different.

BELIEVE WOMEN—those two words sum it all up: women's condition, our experiences with misogyny, and the systemic subversion of our voices. But those words are also inseparable from our dialogues about rape and sexual assault, specifically.

As President Trump put it when he made an equal parts racist and misogynist rape "joke" at a rally in Montana in July 2018, we are, indeed, the "#MeToo generation." The punchline of his "joke" was that this generation is weak, fragile, hypersensitive, and that our movement is somehow steering us toward a radical departure from the toughness of the "real world." But this "#MeToo generation" is more than one single generation: It comprises multiple generations of women and survivors coming forward and raising our voices about our shared experiences. It's a "generation" bound in shared experiences and solidarity, declaring unequivocally that sexual abuse is a systemic issue and one that often stems from disproportionate power dynamics and male dominance across industries.

Predictably enough, this movement hasn't been welcomed by everyone. And during #MeToo's nascence, men who have never experienced assault were swift in their attempts to make the movement about them, and the male perspective, not content to let us finally listen to women's voices. Headline after headline in outlet after outlet spewed out something along the lines of, "#MeToo has made men afraid to hug women," "How #MeToo has made men scared to date," and so on, and so forth, despite how men are statistically more likely to experience sexual assault themselves than be falsely accused of assault.

And we've all heard the men in our lives say it at least once—that being "falsely accused" is the scariest possible thing that could happen to them. Oh, great. The scariest thing that can happen to a woman is being raped and killed.

If you're a man who really believes there's nothing scarier than being falsely accused, perhaps you should consider questioning why, exactly, it is that you believe false reporting happens at all. So that women can come forward and face character attacks, harassment, public humiliation, social ostracism, threats, and disbelief? So they can gain whatever it is that women who publicly discuss sexual violence in society supposedly gain? (Spoiler alert: They gain nothing.)

False reporting of rape is estimated to be in the range of 2 to 8 percent of reports of assaults, although what, exactly, constitutes "false reporting" is hard to say. Most "false reports" involve both parties acknowledging a sexual encounter happened, and simply disputing whether or not one party felt violated by the encounter. Meanwhile, a jarring majority of sexual assaults (between two-thirds and just under 90 percent) are unreported, and that number is likely even higher in reality. The number of women who are silenced by fears of intimidation, harassment, blame, and shame, or fear being forced to relive a traumatic experience through the reporting process, is frankly impossible to quantify. One in five women will be raped in their lives, according to the National Sexual Violence Resource Center. A 2017 survey of heterosexual college-age men revealed most of this demographic still fundamentally misunderstands consent, or don't even realize that acts constituting sexual assault are, in fact, sexual assault.

And yet, nonetheless, media headlines still focused on male insecurity in a new world that is finally starting to hold men accountable, or at least shame them for practicing behaviors that have always been shameful, are gaslighting us into believing that women are now the predators, that women are trying to steal men's freedom and force *them* to live in fear. The irony of men talking about being afraid is that most women are too afraid to go out or walk the streets alone at night, that, every day, women change their walking routes or pay burdensome costs for cabs and Ubers to avoid being cornered and sexually harassed in public.

What women continue to face in this world, across nearly every walk of life, is scary and unfair. We're far from the finish line in terms of gender parity, but our voices and anger in response to this reality continue to be dismissed and trivialized.

The idea that we've already crossed this hypothetical finish line is holding us back from making any real strides toward it—if there even is a finish line at all—and, worse, placing us in abject danger. It's causing us to ignore the women dying from lack of access to reproductive health care, ignore violations of women's free speech, ignore the rampant sexual violence so many women remain too intimidated to speak up about. And none of this should be accepted as normal, or OK, or "not that bad."

WHO'S ALLOWED TO BE ANGRY?

Since the latter half of 2015 and throughout 2016, political truths once buried came to the forefront and became impossible to ignore: the right wing's genuine, uncensored perceptions of women and immigrants and minorities, the crudely intolerant language and blatant lies its leaders would embrace in the name of rejecting "political correctness"—all of it.

Presidential candidate Donald Trump shied away from nothing. His speech announcing his candidacy sweepingly equated Mexican immigrants with rapists and criminals; he turned a blind eye to the numerous mass shootings committed by white men and white supremacists, while never ceding an opportunity to share lies and Islamophobic content on social media in response to cherry-picked terror attacks. Trump suggested punishing women who have abortions, and he dismissed his own documented gloating about committing sexual assault as "locker room talk" before dishing vicious, misogynist character attacks on the dozens of women who accused him of sexual abuse.

His campaign was founded upon and fueled by white male rage—uncensored, unashamed, and terrifying to all the marginalized people subjected to the flood of 24/7 media coverage of it. On occasions too numerous to count while on the campaign trail, he directly encouraged his supporters to commit violence toward protesters who showed up at his rallies, offering to pay his supporters' legal fees if they beat up protesters, and even urging his supporters to attack his political rivals. At one point, Trump seemed to suggest that his supporters use their "Second Amendment rights" and shoot Hillary Clinton. His supporters, who are, mind you, often the same people who demand "due process" and "innocence until proven guilty" for men accused of sexual assault, routinely chant "Lock her up," calling for the jailing of a political rival—and not-so-coincidentally, a woman rival, at that. They proudly donned shirts that read, "She's a cunt, vote for Trump."

The classic, bipartisan explanation of what drove Trump's campaign over the finish line is often "economic anxiety"—forget about how the poorest demographic of Americans (black women) voted for Clinton at a rate of 94 percent, or how 53 percent of voters earning less than $30,000 per year voted for Clinton, compared to 41 percent for Trump, or how 52 percent of voters who regarded the economy as their top concern voted for Clinton, compared to 42 percent for Trump. And forget about all of her thoughtfully crafted, wide-ranging, and unifying economic proposals for affordable and accessible health care, housing, education, and job growth.

Clinton had the audacity to espouse values of diversity and inclusion and talk about her own experience as a woman; and above all, she had the audacity to speak up and run for public office at all as a woman. For many voters, that, in itself, was enough to fuel their rage and send them to the polls in droves for Donald Trump. Somehow, I doubt a single one of them chanting "Lock her up!" could name any real crime she had committed that would warrant jailing; notably, she has yet to be indicted for anything. "Lock her up!" is about punishing women, keeping them in their place—that place being as far away from power and politics as possible—and it's the perfect rallying cry for insecure, slighted, and, above all, angry, white men.

Trump's victory through a flimsy majority of votes in a few, select states served as validation of their anger, just as it served as the dismissal and erasure of everyone else's—that is, the growing majority of the American working class who aren't white men, who live in poverty in coastal urban areas, who are endlessly denied economic opportunity on the basis of identity. Where are the stories validating or even acknowledging their rage? Trump relied heavily on "identity politics"—the politics of white, male anger and resentment, specifically. The only reason we don't call this "identity politics" is that white men have the privilege of being regarded as the default.

It's a popular counter-argument that Trump does not embody the entirety of the Republican Party or conservatism. But this much is true: No matter what Trump said, and no matter how many times Party leadership "disavowed" his choice in words— whatever that even means—the Party stood by him. Party leadership endorsed him, raised money for him, celebrated his win. Almost two years into his presidency, polling revealed President Trump's political party was more united behind the presidency than it had ever been since the World War II era. His electoral victory preceded record numbers of self-identified, proudly racist, white nationalists running for office under the GOP banner, across the country.

The Party has changed in the past three years—perhaps not

so much in its platform and policies, which have always been toxic and wreaked havoc on the lives of women and marginalized people. But specifically, in terms of its efforts to offer some semblance of basic decency, to prioritize some measure of values and courtesy before consolidation of political power, the past three years have seen these past efforts almost wholly eroded with the rise of Trump. Three years of violent speech and bigoted, dehumanizing policy proposals seemed to culminate in one particular 2018 policy that will surely be remembered as among the cruelest, nastiest works of the U.S. government in its modern history: separation of migrant and asylum-seeking families.

At a rate of 45 children separated per day over the course of two months, the federal government ordered border patrol agents to detain and lock up the children and even newborn babies of migrants who had crossed the border, often seeking asylum or safety from rape, gang violence, torture and other human rights abuses south of the border. Separated children were placed in cages in detainment centers, often forced to endure severe weather conditions, and according to numerous documented accusations, at times shackled, beaten, sexually assaulted and otherwise physically abused by state authorities. Pregnant women were denied basic care or forced to sleep on floors, while the Trump administration actively dedicated itself to holding undocumented teenage girls seeking abortion care hostage, even if they were victims of rape.

We heard all kinds of justifications for this policy—that it was merely the enforcement of the law, although which law, exactly, said that children must be ripped from the arms of their parents and locked in cages for trying to flee certain death, no member of the Trump administration was ever quite able to specify. All while ignoring the uptick in white supremacist hate crimes spurred by his rhetoric, the routine gun violence committed by white men, and the prevalence of fatal, racist police brutality, the president hosted rallies for "permanently separated" families, or those who had lost loved ones to violence purportedly committed by immigrants or gang members (who are, to Trump, of course, the same thing). Behind closed doors, the policy was understood as fodder for the Republican Party base ahead of midterms.

Psychologists, medical experts, and other officials who visited child detainment centers all weighed in: Irreparable trauma was being inflicted on children, and gross physical abuses were occurring, all while the president spewed rhetoric equating Central American migrants to vermin and animals, infecting the country with their offensive non-whiteness.

Family separation was supposed to deter them. But it didn't—because how could it? How could it deter people with no other options, fleeing from violence and instability largely created by generations of western recklessness and colonialism throughout Central America? Language barriers, discriminatory hurdles, and lack of resources have made asylum and legal immigration processes all but impossible for families urgently fleeing violence. Family separation was never about incentivizing legal immigration, but punishing people solely for where they come from, for having the audacity to be brown and fight to survive.

Throughout the summer of 2018, with devastating photos of children in cages on full display throughout the internet, and audio of migrant children sobbing after being ripped from their parents blaring in the streets outside Homeland Security Secretary Kirstjen Nielson's home, the discourse began to center around "civility" in politics. You'd think complaints about incivility would be in reference to the jarring, radically inhumane jailing of babies and infliction of mass psychological torture on people whose only crime had been trying to save their children's lives. But rather, outrage over family separation seemed to be matched, if not surpassed, by outrage over how the people responsible for these policies were being treated. Trump administration officials faced heckling, and often loud but never violent protests everywhere they appeared in public.

Even for the age of false equivalences we're living in—one that equated Hillary Clinton, a public servant of 40 years, and her emails, with Donald Trump, an epically incompetent self-admitted sexual predator, and the over a thousand lawsuits against him—this marked a new low. Children were in cages, and media personalities and politicians were comparing Press Secretary Sarah Huckabee Sanders being denied service at restaurants to civil rights and free speech violations shouldered by marginalized people every day. Of course, Sanders was not facing ostracism due to her identity, but her active decision to work for a government that jailed children, and used the jailing of children as a mass, coordinated strategy to discourage an entire group of people from trying to survive.

Nevertheless, the conservative chiding and false equivalences persisted, and all of it—every whiff of it—was gaslighting. The suggestion that yelling at government officials who are guilty of perpetuating a humanitarian crisis was somehow as uncivil as perpetuating a humanitarian crisis, that Americans should see what they know in their hearts is evil and be silent, was gaslighting. Complicity and silence are not civility. Conflating the two, in this case, was meant to normalize a devastating human rights violation, and shame Trump's opponents into ceding the only resource we had to fight back: our voices.

Some of the arguments for civility were so ironic as to be almost humorous—painfully, gut-wrenchingly humorous. A *Washington Post* editorial board decried how liberal activists and citizens could deign to heckle Trump officials, all while their purported counterparts (false equivalences abound), AKA, those tame, comely and perfectly agreeable anti-abortion activists, have the grace to allow abortion providers to live in peace:

> "Those who are insisting that we are in a special moment justifying incivility should think for a moment how many Americans might find their own special moment. How hard is it to imagine, for example, people who strongly believe that abortion is murder deciding that judges or other officials who protect abortion rights should not be able to live peaceably with their families?"

Five measly minutes of research, or listening to women's health providers' voices, would have been all it took for the members of the *Post's* editorial board to see the ridiculousness of this suggestion, but apparently, that was—as it so often is—too much to ask. George Tiller, who, in his lifetime, was the only late-term abortion provider in Kansas, hasn't been dead of assassination by an anti-abortion extremist for quite 10 years. Violence, threats of violence, arson and attempted murders of abortion providers are at a near all-time high in this country, ever since an anti-abortion group released fabricated and illegally obtained videos of Planned Parenthood doctors discussing "selling baby parts" in 2015. And since long before the 2015 videos, anti-abortion protesters have practically lived outside women's health clinics, where they verbally harass patients and clinic staff, to the extent that most clinics across the country recruit special volunteers called clinic escorts to help patients safely enter.

Also in 2015, a couple months after the videos were released, a man who claimed to be a "warrior for the babies" held a Planned Parenthood clinic in Colorado hostage and shot three dead—all while a crowded field of Republican presidential candidates repeatedly decried abortion as the murder of babies. In 2016, the National Network of Abortion Funds' annual nationwide fundraiser was hijacked by anti-abortion hackers, who crashed the fundraising platform, seized the information of donors, and harassed donors and organizers en masse with horrifyingly racist, anti-Semitic, and misogynist language. Renee Bracey Sherman, a vocal reproductive justice activist working with the National Network of Abortion Funds, has spoken out about her experiences with being stalked, doxxed and publicly harassed due to her work as a leader of the reproductive justice movement.

As for Trump cabinet members' right to service, buried in the civility discourse erupting at this time was the story of a woman in Arizona who had been prescribed medication abortion to end an unviable pregnancy, and was turned away by a Walgreens pharmacist who personally opposed abortion. Here was a stark example of someone being discriminated against, publicly humiliated, and denied health care on the basis of her identity. Here was a woman who had had no control over the outcome of her pregnancy being punished nonetheless. Ironically, outrage and buzz about a restaurant turning away Secretary Sanders all but erased this story.

The conversation around civility in this country is fundamentally about who is allowed to be angry, who is allowed to demand respect and be heard, whose dignity and comfort and living standards matter and deserve to be defended and stood up for. This has always been true, and when white male rage was empowered with the highest office in the land on Nov. 8, 2016, this political outcome held a mirror to the inherently oppressive power dynamics of anger and angry behavior in America.

Study after study has shown black men between the ages of 15 and 34 are between nine and 16 times more likely to be killed by police than any other demographic. I first began to pay attention to the news cycle and issues of systemic oppression around the tail-end of 2014, when I was a junior in high school, as protests in Ferguson, Missouri, began to mount in the wake of Michael Brown's tragic, unjust shooting and the exoneration of the police officer who had murdered him. And between then and now, videos of jarring violence and killings targeting unarmed black men are caught on video, circulated for a time on social media, and then simply tucked away at the bottom of a never-ending list of similar incidents, on a near-weekly basis.

None of this is to say communities of color and their allies don't raise their voices, organize, protest and fight back. They show up, and that matters; the erasure of their voices by systemic racism is no fault of theirs. And their mourning, their anger, their frustration in the face of violent injustice and, on their end, often utter helplessness, is policed in a mind-blowingly compassionless manner.

Protests by mourning and rightfully outraged people of

color who have experienced tremendous loss in their communities at the hands of police are regularly portrayed as riots in the media. In April 2018, police arrested Stevante Clark, the brother of an unarmed black man killed by police in his grandmother's backyard for the crime of holding an iPhone while black. Clark was arrested for using "threatening language" directed at police in the wake of his brother's death.

In a country that elected a man who has said the words "grab 'em by the pussy" to the highest office in the land, it's safe to say manners and politeness have never been the priority. Instead, who we choose to listen to and respect regardless of word choice, tone, and semantics is about identity, marginalization, and keeping women and people of color in their place.

At the height of family separation, protesters were screaming in the faces of Trump officials because, as author and *New York Times* columnist Michelle Goldberg put it in a column aptly titled, "We Have a Crisis of Democracy, Not Manners," frankly, it's all we have. "Liberals are using their cultural power against the right because it's the only power they have left, and people have a desperate need to say and to hear others say, that what is happening in this country is intolerable," she wrote.

Goldberg added: "Sometimes, their strategies may be poorly conceived. But there's an abusive sort of victim-blaming in demanding that progressives single-handedly uphold civility, lest the right become even more uncivil in response."

The Republican Party maintains a supermajority in every branch of the federal government and comprises the majority of gubernatorial offices and state legislatures across the country as of 2018. Most of us are just citizens, without any official political decision-making power. We have only our voices and our freedom—enumerated by the First Amendment—to follow our consciences and speak up, speak truth to power. The alternative to being "uncivil," then, is to be silent, and yield quite literally the only power we have to fight back for what we believe in.

Locking children in cages should have marked the end of normalcy in this country—an end created and orchestrated by the right in its choice to defend and stand by Donald Trump. To return what is fundamentally not normal with normal, "civil" behavior is to perpetuate a culture of false equivalence, and normalize what we know is wrong. From the beginning to the end of Trump's family separation policy, that is what the right has demanded of us—and that is what we must never cede them.

AND, NOW, LET'S BE REAL HERE. Calls for civility are rich coming from the same people who stand united under a president who called African and majority non-white countries "shithole" countries and tirelessly defended that comment. Calls for civility are rich coming from the same people who coined the term "political correctness" and branded its negative connotations. That term, which rose to prominence in the 1980s, is meant to make a mockery of basic decency and respect for the experiences of minorities in America, masquerading bullying and bigotry as the courage to say what "real Americans" are thinking. The phrase was adopted to decry a culture of basic decency that says we should ask for pronouns rather than disrespect and erase trans and nonbinary people; a culture that says non-white human beings who come to the United States for either a better life or survival should not be called "illegals"; a culture that says women seeking basic health care like birth control should not be called "sluts."

Of course, there's versatility in how the right discusses "political correctness." More recently, in 2016, then-presidential candidate Ted Cruz called the Pentagon providing gluten-free meals "political correctness." Yes, really.

As a phrase, "political correctness" is a crude laugh in the faces of women, LGBTQ people, people of color, immigrants, and anyone who has the audacity to ask for respect and civility in a country that was not made for them, does not welcome them, and to this day, is not theirs. Above all, it's meant to gaslight us into believing that basic respect and civility—what we're asking for—is somehow asking for far, far too much. But when has this not been the reality? When has the demand for equity and justice, coming from marginalized people, not seemed like too much to ask of society, in the eyes of those who are accustomed to benefiting from inequality? We have always shamed the marginalized for greed, desperation, and asking for too much, simply for asking for what straight, cisgender, white men have always enjoyed.

Of course, often, "political incorrectness" is understood as brave, funny, courageous, and groundbreaking by the right, and even the many liberal-leaning people who sometimes tire of the antics of the "social justice warriors" in their lives. But most sentiments and statements marketed as politically incorrect aren't just *politically* incorrect—they're often also incorrect, plain and simple.

For example, saying immigrants are bringing "rape" and are "criminals" isn't just politically incorrect—as a statement, it's simply incorrect, period. Immigrants are statistically far less likely than native-born citizens to commit crimes. That's just fact, and an easily Googled fact, at that. Nor is this statement somehow partisan—facts may sometimes support the arguments of one side, and, coincidentally, they often support the progressive side. But facts are, at their core, objective.

Another example: In 2012, conservative commentator and evolution-denier Rush Limbaugh used his vast public platform to call a law school student fighting for her school to cover birth control a "slut." Of course, it shouldn't matter remotely how much or how little sex a woman has—everyone has the right to privacy and bodily autonomy, and there is never shame in the sexual lifestyle anyone chooses for themselves. But a reality that conservatives and opponents of reproductive rights so often refuse to acknowledge is that a significant proportion of women also use hormonal birth control for health reasons: to regulate heavy, painful, and sporadic and irregular periods, and to prevent pregnancy that could quite literally kill women with certain health conditions. Many women who use birth control are married, and often even married with children. In other words, despite how it wasn't until the Supreme Court decision *Eisenstadt v. Baird* in 1972 that unmarried women could legally access birth control, birth control doesn't exist solely to enable promiscuity and premarital sex. And if that—promiscuity and premarital sex—*is* what women choose to use birth control for, then so be it.

Saying factually inaccurate, inflammatory things doesn't make you bold, nor does it make you some rebellious maverick who's just saying what everyone else in the room is thinking— that is, as long as you're in a room with vaguely informed, decent people. Anyone who finds themselves calling Mexican immigrants "illegals," or stereotyping Muslim people as "terrorists," or dismissing young women's demands for affordable birth control as whorishness isn't being "politically" incorrect.

In saying any of these things, you're just incorrect—and racist and misogynistic, too.

The people calling for the civil treatment of Trump supporters are the same people who laugh off marginalized people's calls for basic courtesy as excessive "political correctness." They're the same people who encourage the harassment, public humiliation, and dehumanization of trans people with crassly ignorant bathroom laws. It's an utter double standard—and one that, as so many things do, goes back to the fundamental issue of who's allowed to be angry and ask for more in America. The right's abject refusal to acknowledge this double standard is, itself, gaslighting: It's the erasure of all context around why Trump supporters and officials are facing backlash and public resistance, it's the erasure of what real identity-based oppression is, and the normalization of this administration's ongoing war on decency.

Those who work for and publicly, brazenly stand with this administration are owed no decency—not after all that the president and his cabinet have done to perhaps permanently erode decency in society. If anything, they are owed public, loud outcry.

It's as simple as this: We can't treat them as if what they're doing is normal. No liberal leaders, not even Rep. Maxine Waters in her glorious, controversial speech that encouraged all decent people to speak up and protest any Trump official they see in public, have ever called for violence directed at supporters or members of this administration. That's a far cry from President Trump's direct incitements of violence as a candidate, his very public defenses of numerous men and politicians serially accused of sexual assault and domestic violence (he, himself, has been accused of marital rape, and assaulting more than 20 women), or the repeated incidents of women being sexually assaulted at his campaign rallies between 2015 and 2016. In one particularly unsettling incident in Wisconsin, a 15-year-old girl was sexually assaulted and then pepper sprayed by a group of Trump supporters.

Violence directed at Trump supporters does happen—but it happens not out of racial resentment, like the Trump supporters who assaulted and urinated on a homeless Mexican man in 2015 in Trump's name (an act that Trump took his sweet time disavowing), but out of rage that is, in itself, justified by this administration's proactive, intolerant cruelty. And there is nothing to link these occasional episodes of anti-Trump violence to words by Democratic or liberal leaders.

Ultimately, the right's precious "civility" is rooted in a false narrative. Sure, they're correct that in recent years, we've seen escalated violence and incivility in our politics. But it's coming from the very people who have the audacity to posture themselves as victims.

IN THE VEIN OF MOCKING MARGINALIZED people for asking for too much, there's also the issue of how young women, in particular, are portrayed for either advocating for their rights, or on behalf of other marginalized people. The terms "social justice warrior" and "feminazi" have become staples of right-wing internet vernacular, peppered across *Breitbart*, *The Daily Caller*, *The Federalist* and *Townhall* articles and Reddit threads. Even self-identified liberals often float the term "SJW" in reference to people who talk about social justice issues more loudly, or just a little more often than some liberal-leaning people are comfortable with. And no one is called an SJW or feminazi more often than young women.

The term social justice warrior itself isn't necessarily mocking young women for caring; the premise of the term is that young women would only ever speak up for or express their opinions for attention, or, essentially, validation from men and patriarchal institutions. Thus, it operates on the assumption that young women have no real opinions, that everything they say about issues of social justice is self-righteous posturing and the stroking of their own moral egos for attention.

In a similar vein, women protesters who flood the Capitol, the Supreme Court, and organize rallies like the Women's March across the country to stand up for human rights issues, from the family separation policy to the right to health care, are often dismissed as professional "paid actors" by President Trump and other Republican leaders. This accusation by Republicans and the president was especially repeated in the face of mass, women-led opposition to Trump's Supreme Court nominee Brett Kavanaugh in the summer and fall of 2018. Apparently, our male leaders cannot even fathom that women have the capacity to form our own opinions and stand up for them.

Of course, women and especially young women are also mocked for genuinely caring and bringing attention to issues that are traditionally ignored. Just like many Democrats and liberal Americans, until Election Day rolls around, most young women have virtually zero options for real recourse, nor any real political power other than through raising our voices wherever and whenever we can. Most young women are not elected officials, and lack national influence and far-reaching public profiles. We see what's happening and care too much to do nothing;

and subsequently, all we really can do is speak up on any and all social media platforms, in any and all conversations. In many ways, speaking up is all we really have in our arsenal, and so of course we do it. We speak up not out of weakness or what the right often calls "self-victimization," but out of strength, to call out sexism and oppression and refuse to turn a blind eye to it.

If your impulse is to feel anger at someone for utilizing their only meaningful option to make positive change, consider the underlying reasons for your anger. Consider the underlying gendered animus in finding angry, outspoken and opinionated young women annoying and dismissible. Consider why it is that when men show anger about an issue, or speak from a place of passion, they are rewarded with recognition and acknowledgment of their authenticity, and even come off as more "likable."

The outrage of young women is itself outrageous. The outrage of young women, to have the audacity to not settle for the world as it is and demand more, demand better—for themselves and for all—is outrageous in patriarchy.

ANYTHING YOUNG WOMEN ASK FOR that expands beyond the status quo, even if it's so simple as to not be sexually assaulted, is often made into a joke by proponents of "political incorrectness." In July 2018, President Trump held a rally in Montana during which he reiterated his tired jokes about Massachusetts Sen. Elizabeth Warren's claims of having some Native American heritage. Then, seeming to confuse DNA tests with rape kits, the President of the United States said before a roaring crowd: "I'm going to get one of those little kits and in the middle of the debate, when [Warren] proclaims she's of Indian heritage... We will take that little kit, but we have to do it gently, because we're in the 'Me Too' generation, so we have to be very gentle."

The punchline of that "joke" was that #MeToo has made fragile snowflakes of us all. The punchline of that joke was women who have literally survived sexual violence, but still find the bravery to speak up and stand up for other survivors. Following the logic of Trump's "joke," asking to not be assaulted and for people who commit acts of sexual abuse to be held accountable is somehow a tall ask and display of weakness to Trump and his base of "real Americans."

And, of course, young women aren't just mocked and derided for caring. They're also discredited and condescended to whenever they may choose to speak up and take stances on issues, in general. Upon using social media to bring attention to issues of oppression, we're often criticized for exaggerating the issue—no matter how many stats we cite—whether we're talking about the gender wage gap, or the prevalence of sexual assault, or the new extremes of the war on reproductive rights. And that gendered, fundamental demand of patriarchal gaslighting—that we "prove it"—belies this criticism.

As one example, young women's social media posts about the wage gap continue to be met with condescending commentary—often from people who purport to not be sexists, but just "reasonables" and "contrarians." They argue that the gap exists solely because women "choose to be English majors," ignoring how within STEM work, the wage gap stands between roughly 11 and 30 percent. But, hey, *details*. Our posts about sexual assault are met with skeptical comments about how we're undermining America's "innocent until proven guilty" judicial foundations. And unsurprisingly, these comments fail to list any suggestions for how survivors, the vast majority of whom—believe it or not—were not wearing body cameras while being assaulted, could actually "prove" their experiences in a manner that would satiate institutions built to doubt and disbelieve women.

Additionally, young women's advocacy about abortion rights is often met with the same cynicism and accusations of exaggeration, solely because abortion has been legal on the federal level since 1973. Of course, the reality is that legality has failed to yield access for all; access to abortion has been gutted across the country by a wide range of medically unnecessary, harmful and discriminatory restrictions on abortion. The dire situation around reproductive rights in this country, especially with developments in the Supreme Court as of the summer of 2018, is impossible to exaggerate—not when more women die of pregnancy or birth-related complications in the U.S. than in any other industrialized country, and not with such a clear correlation between higher numbers of maternal deaths and more state-level restrictions on abortion.

The oppression women face is real, and the oppression that we talk about—whether we face it ourselves or stand as allies to LGBTQ people, people of color, the differently abled, and other marginalized groups—is, too. Additionally, while most evidence is anecdotal, there is also significant empirical evidence of how the political rise of Donald Trump, which has vastly affected and threatened the rights of all marginalized people, has simultaneously and negatively affected mental health in the U.S. In the final weeks leading up to Election Day in 2016—even before Trump won—52 percent of respondents said they felt stressed by presidential campaigning. Sixty-three percent said they felt stressed about the future of the nation, and among Democrats, this number was substantially higher at 73 percent.

None of this should be surprising. For many Americans, the election of either Hillary Clinton or Donald Trump meant the difference between staying in the U.S., and being forced to leave the only country they'd ever known. It meant losing health insurance, or their ability to access the resources that empower them to control their bodies. It meant losing the right to marry who they love, the rights to not be discriminated against by landlords and employers on the basis of gender and sexuality.

It's no surprise the people who mock political correctness and "social justice warriors" are often the same people who deride safe spaces and trigger warnings as comedic spoofs. After all, they only take mental health seriously—or pretend to—when doing so allows them to pivot from questions about common-sense gun control. Outside of the scope of gun violence, they continue to ignore how their trivialization of marginalized people's experiences almost certainly contributes to the national mental health epidemic.

All while slashing protections for affordable, accessible mental health care, further stigmatizing mental illness by associating it with mass shooters (people with mental illnesses are far more likely to be victims than perpetrators of violence), and perpetuating oppressive policies and rhetoric that negatively impact marginalized people's mental health, right-wing politicians, do, indeed, speak about mental health often. But that's only because mass shootings *happen* often, and due to their legislative inaction, no less.

The next time they bring up mental health in response to a

mass shooting—which, tragically, will inevitably roll around again—let's not forget all the times they criticized or joked about the coddling of "social justice warriors," or joked about trigger warnings and safe spaces.

WHO ARE WE WILLING TO LISTEN TO? Who are we willing to take seriously? Whose demands for respect and civility matter?

The right is willing to uplift and pay attention to the voices of some members of marginalized groups, but it's important to recognize that by no means does this counter their well-earned reputation for intolerance and bigotry.

The Trump administration may comprise the most white, male cabinet in recent U.S. history, but it has its Ivankas and Kellyannes and Kirstjens. It has its resident Ben Carson, and is happy to tout token supporters when convenient, as well. At the end of the day, the only people the right adores almost as much as straight white men are the women and people of color who are, for whatever reason, satisfied with what rights rich, white male politicians so generously choose to confer upon them.

Fundamentally, who we choose to listen to is often a matter of respectability politics. And when I say respectability politics, I'm referring to the tendency to exclusively listen to and advance the most traditionally "respectable" members of marginalized groups, or those who have internalized or accepted blame for their oppression, and therefore do not cause trouble for people with privilege. This political approach fundamentally ignores all the other members of marginalized groups who fail to adequately conform or accept blame for their circumstances. It ignores the stories of those who weren't able to "pull themselves up by their bootstraps," those who continue to face dire, existential threats to their existence simply because of the circumstances into which they were born.

And unfortunately, the right isn't necessarily alone in playing this game.

For example, affirmative action, while crucial to protecting diversity in higher education and proactively combating the continuation of generations of inequality, more or less reflects respectability politics, as Michelle Alexander has suggested in her book *The New Jim Crow*. In many communities of color across the country, issues like the racist school-to-prison pipeline, sex trafficking, police brutality, and substance abuse can often pose more dire threats than college attendance, and whether or not one will receive admission into an Ivy League. Affirmative action may support the most traditionally "respectable" members of minority communities but will leave behind just about everyone else in these groups.

More relevant to the issue of gaslighting and young women, consider for a moment why young vocal feminists draw so much ire, backlash, and condescension for expressing their opinions. Because they're women, and they're loud, hard to swallow, and refuse to internalize and accept blame for their oppression. They decline to stay in the lane paved for them by our nation's patriarchal history, and its persistently patriarchal present.

It's unfair that we have to tell young women to prepare for mockery, harassment, and public shaming simply for being young women and expressing their opinions. It's unfair that women aren't included in that narrow, predominantly male bloc of people whose voices and demands for civility are heard and respected. But it's the reality. And it's the reason that, for all the ridicule and portrayals of young feminists as weak, sensitive, and fragile simply for caring, I know women and girls are the strong ones—we've had to be, not only to participate in society but also, ultimately, to survive and be heard.

"PROVE IT": MIGRAINES, BIRTH CONTROL, AND THE ABORTION RAPE EXCEPTION

In February 2018, *Vogue* told a story of Serena Williams that few had heard before—a story few had heard, but far too many women of color have lived.

Williams recalled a string of near life-threatening complications after giving birth to her first child, daughter Alexis Olympia, in 2017. Specifically, after having a Cesarean section, Williams struggled with embolisms, blood clots and a rupture in her C-section wound that had made it difficult to breathe. She would wind up having multiple surgeries to save her life, before eventually returning home and being put on six-weeks bedrest. But part of the reason that what had started with Williams feeling short of breath after giving birth quickly spiraled into such a dangerous situation had been the lack of proper care Williams received after she had first reported her pain and discomfort to her nurse.

As per the *Vogue* feature, it went down like this::

> "[Williams] walked out of the hospital room so her mother wouldn't worry and told the nearest nurse, between gasps, that she needed a CT scan with contrast

and IV heparin (a blood thinner) right away. The nurse thought her pain medicine might be making her confused. But Serena insisted, and soon enough a doctor was performing an ultrasound of her legs. 'I was like, a Doppler? I told you, I need a CT scan and a heparin drip,' she remembers telling the team. The ultrasound revealed nothing, so they sent her for the CT, and sure enough, several small blood clots had settled in her lungs. Minutes later she was on the drip. 'I was like, listen to Dr. Williams!'"

Despite how Williams had had a history with life-threatening embolisms and specifically underwent surgery for this in 2011, when she initially reported her experiences post-birth, she was met with disbelief—disbelief that may have put her life in danger, and delayed her receiving crucial care.

Even as a wealthy, high-profile black woman, due to persistent racial bias in health care, the act of giving birth had almost killed her.

Black women are 243 percent more likely than white women to die from pregnancy or childbirth-related causes in the United States, a country that already has the highest maternal mortality rate in the industrialized world, with an average of 26.4 deaths per 100,000 live births. That number increases to 44 per 100,000 for black women and shrinks to 13 for white women, and 14 for women of other races, according to data from the Centers for Disease Control and Prevention. According to researchers, 50,000 women in America face life-threatening pregnancy-related complications annually, and black women are three to four times more likely than white women to die from these complications.

Of course, there are many factors that contribute to the United States' outlandishly high maternal mortality rate, and one of those is the mounting trend of oppressive, medically unnecessary abortion restrictions that have swept across the country in recent years. Between 2011 and 2016, about 27 percent of all roughly 1,200 abortion restrictions enacted since *Roe v. Wade* (1973) were passed. In states where there are more restrictions on abortion, such as South Carolina, in particular, women are substantially more likely to die of pregnancy-related causes.

In 2015, South Carolina's maternal mortality rate increased by 300 percent, after lawmakers in the state and then-Gov. Nikki Haley signed off on several of the most extreme abortion laws in the country, including "restrictions on insurance coverage for abortion, limits on which healthcare professionals can perform abortions, mandatory counseling on fetal pain and development, and requirements on the time frame within which abortion can be performed," according to a 2017 report by the Center for Reproductive Rights. The next year, Haley signed a law banning abortion at 20-weeks, despite how fewer than 10 percent of all abortions take place after the first trimester, and in these rare situations, the pregnancy is often unviable or unsafe. In other words, anti-abortion restrictions constitute a massive public health issue.

Additionally, abortion restrictions and their indisputable relationship with maternal death are, in many ways, an economic issue, especially in light of a federal law (the Hyde amendment) that prohibits federal funding from paying for elective abortion, and laws in 32 states that restrict insurance coverage of abortion. And the economic implications of this issue are far from race-neutral.

One particularly draconian example of this exists in the Trump administration's policy of imprisoning pregnant undocumented minors who seek elective abortions, or even abortion for pregnancy that is the result of rape. Between 60 and 80 percent of Central American migrant women and girls who cross the U.S. border experience sexual assault, and in 2018, border patrol officers reported the prevalence of minors as young as 12-years-old being put on birth control pills before traveling across the border in anticipation of rape.

The militarization of the border, actively supported by the Trump administration, is a key factor in why sexual assault is so prevalent for migrant women and girls at the border and en route to it. In either case, despite repeatedly losing lawsuits regarding its treatment of migrant women and girls seeking abortion, Trump's Office of Refugee Resettlement has persisted in its behavior. In courts, the Justice Department has repeatedly claimed non-citizens do not share the same rights as citizens, nor are they entitled to human rights, to justify its cruelty.

In the summer of 2018, in the weeks following President Trump's executive order to end his family separation policy and replace it with one of indefinite incarceration for migrant families, several migrant women filed a lawsuit alleging grave abuse, and claims that being denied medical care and shackled at the stomach while pregnant had induced miscarriages and endangered their lives. These atrocities were notably committed at the behest of a "pro-life" administration.

The aforementioned policies specifically affect immigrant women and girls, but other women of color face explicitly racist laws around abortion and reproductive health, too. Women's state prison populations in America grew 834 percent over nearly 40 years since 1978, which is more than double the pace of growth among male prison populations, and women of color comprise a majority of incarcerated women. Incarcerated pregnant women are vulnerable to face the same radically inhumane conditions of detained pregnant migrant women and girls.

But even among non-incarcerated women of color, horror stories of poverty and racial bias in health care abound on a life-threatening level.

Women as a whole are 35 percent more likely than men to live in poverty, according to a report by the National Women's Law Center from 2015. But compared to 9.6 percent of white women, 23.1 and 22.7 percent of black and Latinx women, respectively, live in poverty. In 2013, researchers found black women were substantially more likely than white women to be uninsured.

In other words, the disparity in resources along racial lines is, without a doubt, a key threat to the living standards of women of color, particularly in the realm of pregnancy and childbirth. Even today—or perhaps, especially today—it's worth remembering that a decisive majority of the women of pre-*Roe v. Wade* America who had unsafe, sometimes fatal abortions were immigrants and women of color, and speaking more broadly, low-income women who couldn't afford the costs to travel to have safe abortions in the states where it was legal. In the 1960s, between 200,000 and 1.2 million unsafe abortions took place in the U.S. every year, according to Guttmacher Institute, and thousands of women died as a result of this. And as of 2018, in light of modern, severe threats to *Roe* with a conservative-majority Supreme Court, judicial system stacked with anti-choice judges, and state legislatures brimming with radically repressive abortion bills, this history feels all the more relevant.

In either case, as Serena Williams' experiences indicate, the disparity in pregnancy and birth conditions between white women and women of color exists even for wealthy and influential women of color. And that's because the underlying racial biases in health care aren't always contingent on one's economic situation.

————————————

SYSTEMIC OPPRESSION IS unfailingly intersectional, but it's critical to understand the gender biases that exist in our health care system before we can fully understand the experiences of women of color. The dismissal and trivialization of women's pain where health care is concerned are an unspoken truth women live with every day. Stereotyping women as inherently weaker and more sensitive than men means that our complaints of pain and discomfort, and our fears about our health and wellbeing, are treated with a too-often fatal grain of salt by doctors.

It wasn't until the latter part of the 20th century that women were even allowed to go to doctor's appointments without the presence of a male guardian, and the presumption that women still cannot credibly speak for ourselves, or be trusted to accurately represent our own condition and experiences, persists to this day.

These presumptions exist foremost in how we're often asked to prove our pain in ways that we simply can't, or are gaslit by our doctors into believing that what we're experiencing is normal. The burden of proof placed on women seeking care is inextricably bound to the popular narrative that women and girls make up their experiences "for attention" in patriarchal society. It's a narrative that, among other things, has helped yield devastatingly high rates of non-reporting in cases of sexual violence against women, who fear coming forward and being accused of telling lies "for attention." Additionally, despite perceptions of women as weak, women are substantially more likely to endure severe threats to our physical and mental health, and endure these conditions without complaint because of the internalized perception that our experience is not severe enough to come forward and seek care.

The reasons women suffer physical ailments, from the often quite literally nauseating side effects of hormonal birth control, to the gendered epidemic of migraines, in silence, are similar to the reasons that anywhere from 62 to 84 percent of all sexual assaults are unreported. Women are painfully aware of the culture of misogyny we live in—a culture that routinely humiliates and endangers us by neglecting to take our pain seriously, or believe us when we say that we're in pain.

One stark example of this is the disproportionate prevalence of migraines among women. This is, in part, biological. But this epidemic is also so vast and widely untreated because of systemic gaslighting of women and girls by doctors, as well as a culture that trivializes and erases our pain. I don't have a single female friend who doesn't carry Advil or Tylenol in her purse, not just because of menstrual cramps, but also in no small part due to recurring headaches: headaches that we're expected to weather without complaint, and regard as normal. It's not uncommon for older women to advise young women to describe severe abdominal cramps to their doctors as the feeling of being stabbed, just to be taken seriously.

But women who do have the audacity to question their living conditions and demand health and comfort often face skepticism and dismissal. Thirty-six million Americans, including 18 percent of all adult women, regularly experience migraines—and this stat only includes women who actually report experiencing migraines. Despite these numbers, as of 2018, there's still no real, long-term cure for migraines, and this reality can't be divorced from the stereotype that women are weak, overly sensitive, and exaggerate our experiences.

The trivialization of women's pain often results in general disadvantage: in our schooling, our careers, our ability to publicly participate in society. The constraints on women's ability to care for ourselves and lead healthy lives means missing class or work—and the loss of income that comes with jobs that don't offer paid time off—due to severe migraines, menstrual cramping, or nausea from birth control, all of which are experiences that men are less likely to or don't suffer from at all. For former Republican presidential candidate Michelle Bachmann, who famously suffered from recurring migraines, it meant disadvantage against her male rivals who didn't have to take time off to recover and rest from migraines.

Another stark reality that is inextricably bound to expectations for women to prove our pain is the gendered double standard in the living standards that men and women are allowed to ask for in the patriarchy.

Amid ongoing attacks on women's right to access birth control without facing discrimination from pharmacists, insurers, and employers, the past few years have been peppered with developments and advancements in male hormonal birth control. While I can't quite delve into the mechanics of the EP055 compound and how it functions to demobilize sperm, what I can and will delve into is the long, often ironically sexist history of birth control. As a disclaimer, I fully support women's right to choose hormonal birth control pills—God only knows how many women have been empowered to live meaningful, autonomous lives through the ability to dodge unwanted pregnancy and be healthy. But what I will say is that we should never forget female birth control's inception, and how it compares with dramatically more humane modern experiments to create male birth control.

The first female birth control was tested on human women: Puerto Rican women and women with disabilities, specifically. In contrast, for the past few years, male birth control experiments have almost exclusively been conducted on male monkeys, with the exception of a 2016 World Health Organization study that eventually went to trial on male subjects after extensive testing. However, Stage II of the experiment was almost immediately canceled due to "safety reasons" after an independent review panel determined the hormonal injection for men had too many side effects—namely, the side effects prevalent in most female birth control methods, such as nausea, depression, mood instability, effects on libido, acne, and others. At the time, NPR reported that the majority of the trial's 320 male subjects dropped out, claiming to be unable to withstand the side effects that millions of women around the world experience every day.

The allocation of burden and responsibility in preventing pregnancy has always been sexist in and of itself due to the expectation that women alone should be the ones to shoulder the physical discomfort of birth control side effects to prevent pregnancy. It's emblematic of who in society is allowed to ask for more—and who isn't.

As of 2018, researchers in the United States have already developed symptom-less *male* birth control; varying versions of this product are already on the market—and cheap, at just $10 a pop—in India. And yet, because of the long tradition of women exclusively being responsible for preventing pregnancy, male birth control may never go to market in the U.S., simply because experts predict investors in the pharmaceutical industry will always simply assume there is no interest in male birth control. In 2018, an all-female team of researchers at the University of Minnesota said obtaining funding for their research of male birth control was often a struggle, "because the drug industry already has effective options for women, [so] it's underestimated interest in a pill for men."

Simply put, women who suffer from side effects from their birth control should not have to carry this burden—especially when long-term, reliable and symptom-free options exist for men to prevent pregnancy. We shouldn't have to accept nausea, mood swings and general discomfort and physical and mental instability as an everyday norm. We shouldn't have to choose between preventing pregnancy in order to meet professional and academic goals, and our comfort. And we shouldn't be placed in a position where our wellness is reduced to collateral damage, just so we can have safe, healthy sex and participate in society.

There's a different burden of proof for men and women's pain. As the aforementioned birth control experiments demonstrate, men and women can quite literally face the same conditions—but only men's experiences will be acknowledged and taken seriously. And the consequences of this double standard, throughout history and today, have been devastating.

FOR WOMEN OF COLOR, there are a couple of crucial caveats to all of this.

In the United States and all western societies, there is a long history of selectively caring about rape and violence against women if and only if it applies to white women, and perpetuates stereotypes about black and brown men as violent, bestial and dangerous. In Donald Trump's 2015 speech announcing his presidential candidacy, he called Mexican immigrants "rapists" and murderers and repeatedly used alleged sexual violence committed by immigrant men as a talking point. Within two years, he would impose a policy of keeping detained, pregnant migrant rape victims incarcerated for seeking abortion care as president.

There's a message here beyond surface-level, run-of-the-mill racism and nativism. The stereotype of fragile, delicate white femininity and the notion that this must be protected at all costs perhaps impacts who is perceived as needing and deserving of better care, and whose health scares are treated with more urgency. In contrast, dehumanizing tropes comparing black women to apes, and portrayals of them as inherently more "masculine" than their white women counterparts, could also play a role in black women's disparate experiences with pregnancy-related health risks and maternal death. The jarring disparities in maternal deaths and life-threatening pregnancy complications affecting women of color make clear the extent to which racial bias has infected our health care system, and in the U.S., women of color are suffering the consequences of this en masse.

Women of color face another grave threat to their safety and rights when it comes to pregnancy: the risk of being punished for the outcome of their pregnancy. Especially in light of the story of a woman who miscarried being denied medication abortion by a Walgreens pharmacist on the grounds of "religious freedom" in the summer of 2018, we know miscarriage and abortion are conflated all too often, especially because anti-abortion politicians and groups are often staunchly anti-science, too. The story of Purvi Patel, an Indiana woman who was jailed for almost a full year due to the outcome of her pregnancy, offers a harrowing glimpse of what women could face as a consequence for miscarrying or attempting to terminate a pregnancy.

In 2013, Patel checked herself into a hospital seeking help for uninterrupted bleeding, saying she had given birth to a stillborn fetus. When doctors noticed the size of her umbilical cord, they became suspicious the fetus had actually been born alive, and eventually found its discarded remains in a dumpster where Patel confessed to having discarded them.

She would wind up being arrested and charged with two contradictory charges: fetal homicide, and neglect of a child. The charges were puzzling because neglecting a child means that you neglected a *live* child, while feticide means that the baby was born dead. A jury managed to find her guilty of both.

The basis of the child neglect charge had been a widely discredited "lung float test" which prosecutors used to determine that her fetus had been able to breathe and was 25 to 30 weeks along—a far cry from the 23 to 24 weeks that Patel's lawyers had proven by demonstrating the fetus' lungs were not sufficiently developed to breathe. The results of the lung float test suggested the baby had been alive, and "killed" by Patel's neglect. Meanwhile, the basis of the feticide charge had been text messages obtained by police in which Patel seemed to discuss buying abortifacient to attempt to terminate the pregnancy, but no trace of the drug had even been found in her blood work.

The following year, three judges on an appeals court exonerated Patel, but the incident nevertheless reflects the serious threat posed by abortion opponents' inability to draw substantive, science-based and consistent lines around what constitutes life. The state feticide law that the prosecution had used to put Patel behind bars was not meant to punish women who have self-managed abortions, but rather, people—namely domestic abusers—who commit violent acts against pregnant women. In the same vein, the state's use of the pseudoscience lung float test to "prove" the fetus had actually been a live baby shows how false science is often dangerously used to humanize fetuses, dehumanize pregnant women by exposing them to the possibility of criminal charges for the outcomes of their pregnancies, and jeopardize women's health and wellness.

We may never really, fully know what happened to Patel's pregnancy; her text messages and actual examinations of her physical condition tell different stories. But that's neither here nor there. What we do know is that Patel lived with conservative, pro-abstinence parents and her hesitation to divulge a complete account of her experiences likely came from a place of deep fear about her safety.

For years, stereotypes of Asian women as likely to abort or commit feticide or infanticide on the basis of the fetus' gender have yielded racist, innocuous state laws across the country (for example, laws that ban abortion on the basis of the fetus' gender or race). And in addition to pervasive, systemic discrimination that renders women of color more likely than white women to be charged with crimes or incarcerated in general, the stereotype of the "baby-killing" Asian woman poses a unique danger for those who become pregnant, and either experience complications or seek to terminate the pregnancy.

Before Patel, there was another Asian-American Indiana woman who faced more than a year in jail for miscarrying after a failed suicide attempt while she had been pregnant. In 2011, after being impregnated by a man who was not her husband, Bei Bei Shuai, a Chinese immigrant, attempted to take her own life by consuming rat poison. She survived, but her 33-week-old fetus did not, and required a Caesarian section to be removed. She faced similar feticide charges, as well as a murder charge, and was jailed for 435 days before the Indiana Supreme Court cleared the charges against her.

Varying versions of the stories of Patel and Shuai exist in states across the country with more repressive cultures around abortion. They reflect a reality of women, and disproportionately women of color, being doubly punished for their pain and trauma, and, in so many words, told that unviable, miscarried fetuses are more valuable than they are, and have more rights and legal protection than they do as living women. The fight for bodily autonomy for women did not end with *Roe v. Wade*, and it's the very notion this is the case that's allowed incidents like the incarceration of Patel and Shuai to arise. *Roe v. Wade* was not the end of criminalized abortion, and if we allow ourselves to be gaslit into believing this, to be lulled into a false sense of security, stories like this will continue to unfold under our nose.

The bodies and wellbeing of women of color remain not only disproportionately neglected but also disproportionately policed within our health care and legal systems. And the direct results of this include vastly disproportionate maternal and pregnancy-related death rates for women of color, and a dangerous, draconian application of laws that were created with the intention of protecting pregnant women.

WOMEN—and especially low-income women, women of color, and immigrant women—are marginalized within the American health care system through its routine dismissal of their pain. And the biases, misogyny, and racism that are costing women across the country their lives exist everywhere—especially in politics. Certainly, these attitudes are more prevalent among the white Republican men who have devoted their political careers fighting for nearly every restriction on abortion access you could name. But watered down anti-women biases also exist even within those liberal and progressive spaces.

In 2018, just months before midterm elections, I had the pleasure of speaking with the founders of the American Women's Party for a feature I was writing. One particularly enlightening moment of our conversation tackled progressive men and how the exclusion of women even from progressive spaces and discussions hurts women, too. According to the American Women's Party, without women in the room, our rights and experiences remain an afterthought at best. "It's always, 'Well, let's worry about health care and we'll include reproductive rights after' … This idea that they [male lawmakers] were ever going to consider us or put our issues on the same playing field hasn't worked, even for the more compassionate male legislators," Maya Contreras, one founder of the organization, said. "We have seen unequivocally that if you don't have those women in the room, or making those policy decisions, they'll just be left out."

One well-known example of this exists in the internal war among Democrats that saw proactive measures to protect and expand abortion access ultimately removed from the writing of the Affordable Care Act. But this wasn't just one isolated episode or an anomaly of some sort. Think about progressive icon Sen. Bernie Sanders' embrace of tuition-free public college, and question why universal child care and similar measures that address traditionally feminine experiences remain excluded from mainstream progressive dialogues and widely regarded as fringe.

In recent years, under the Trump administration and a Republican-majority Congress, we have seen an escalation in preexisting conditions being used to disproportionately attack women and relegate womanhood itself to a preexisting condition, with disastrous consequences for rape survivors in particular. Pregnancy, being a mother, having had an abortion, and, yes, surviving sexual assault and domestic violence, could all be used as grounds for insurance providers to raise premiums or turn women away altogether.

Defending protections for people with preexisting conditions has long been a talking point of Democrats, but one that seldom goes so far as to recognize Republican policies as direct attacks on womanhood. As Slate's Christina Cauterucci put it in 2018, the culmination of the GOP's attacks on affordable health care and reproductive rights reflect "a medical framework that [treats] women's bodies as inherently sick, aberrations from the norm"—a medical framework of abject, misogyny-fueled cruelty.

And the punishment of rape survivors in politics and medicine is as egregious as it is pervasive. Senate Republicans' rejection of renewing the Violence Against Women Act in 2013, and the devastating consequences that dismantling the VAWA would have had for women of color, Native American women, LGBTQ people and other marginalized identities disproportionately affected by sexual violence, couldn't be understated. Luckily, of course, VAWA lived. But rape survivors continue to encounter systemic gaslighting and abuse in health care through restrictions on abortion that exist across the country.

Many of the most extreme bills and laws to restrict or explicitly ban abortion offer exceptions for women whose pregnancies threaten their lives, are unviable, or are the result of rape. This last item is known as the rape exception.

Of course, due to their extreme nature, many of these bills fail to be enacted. But that said, women who live in the (as of 2018) 17 states with 20-week abortion bans and the 32 states that prohibit insurance coverage of abortions except in cases of rape, and whose pregnancies are among the 25,000 per year in the U.S. that are the result of rape, are severely affected by the rape exception and its cruelty nonetheless.

Let's be clear: The rape exception is not about helping women, whose right to reproductive freedom should not be contingent on how they became pregnant, nor whether they are able to successfully prove to law enforcement, doctors, or anyone else that they were sexually abused. The rape exception is self-serving propaganda for anti-choice, anti-women politicians, and the complete and utter gaslighting of women and survivors. It's about manipulating the optics of abortion policy to make abortion bans appear more humane and digestible to mainstream audiences, all while sending the toxic and false message that rape can easily be proven, that anyone who is impregnated by rape could easily come forward, say they were raped, and receive appropriate care, simple as that.

Of course, the reality is that women and survivors who come forward about being sexually assaulted comprise a distinctly small minority. Among the many reasons survivors choose not to come forward, which include choosing to heal and move on privately on their own terms (an option the rape exception would deprive them of) is fear of intimidation, disbelief, and being shamed or blamed. When we require women to sacrifice their privacy and comfort, and potentially force them to relive a traumatic experience just to access health care like abortion, we deny them autonomy in their recovery process, and certainly strip them of bodily autonomy, too, by making theirs conditional.

If anything, the rape exception arguably makes things worse for women by repressing our rights and threatening our safety, all while allowing anti-choice politicians to humanize their agenda within the mainstream, and affirm a false narrative about what survivors of sexual assault face in coming forward.

According to the most recent polling, an estimated 16 percent of Americans believe abortion should be illegal without any exception, even for rape. During GOP Congressman Todd Akin's race for U.S. Senate in 2012, Akin dismissed the possibility of pregnancy by rape by citing religious pseudoscience about how "legitimate rape" cannot result in pregnancy, and therefore, abortion should not be legal in any circumstances. Views like his and the other 16 percent of Americans who unilaterally believe abortion should be illegal are appalling. But don't allow any GOP lawmaker, as they desperately peddle out bill after bill to restrict or ban abortions except in cases of rape, to gaslight you into believing that they or their laws are somehow any *less* appalling.

The rape exception is not a good thing. It does not make bans on abortion safer or less cruel, inhumane, and likely to result in women being subjected to unsafe abortions; it's not a compromise. That's because there is no compromise on abortion; nothing keeps women—and sexual assault survivors—safe except a full, unconditional range of safe, legal health care options.

The phenomenon of women being forced to prove their pain for health care in ways that men are not is inseparable from the rape exception and its devastating consequences. Reproductive rights and violence against women are interconnected, inseparable issues. Erasing or dismissing women's pain and health struggles; banning abortion and birth control access; and committing sexual assault are all extreme acts of violence on women's bodies that disregard our consent and safety.

THE KENNEDY VACANCY AND ABORTION

On June 26, 2018, Supreme Court Justice Anthony Kennedy announced his retirement. I was working as an intern at one of the biggest reproductive rights groups in the country at the time, and the moment the news broke, the office became a blur of nonstop rapid response; there wasn't a free moment, the phone line rang incessantly across every department—it was, without a doubt, the most chaotic and jarring day of my life, perhaps since Election Day in 2016.

To be clear, Anthony Kennedy was not a liberal, nor a champion of women's rights. His announcement came just days after he had voted to uphold President Trump's nakedly Islamophobic, xenophobic "travel ban," and had dealt critical blows to unions, voting rights, and, in a case about fake women's health clinics, women's rights. But over the course of his 30-year career, he consistently served as a swing vote that brought balance to the high court in times of blistering polarization. And, more important than feel-good narratives about nonpartisanship, he acted as the key vote to uphold and protect *Roe v. Wade*, and with it, safe legal abortion on the federal level.

When the Supreme Court was one vote away from reversing two decades of progress and overturning *Roe* in 1992 with

Planned Parenthood v. Casey, Kennedy's vote saved reproductive freedom. In 2015, his vote made marriage equality the law of the land. And in 2016, he effectively saved abortion access, siding with abortion providers who were being phased out by discriminatory laws in *Whole Women's Health v. Hellerstedt*.

His retirement threatened all of that. At the time of Kennedy's retirement, perhaps Trump would be gone in the next few years, barring a 2020 election victory. But his Supreme Court Justice would serve a lifetime and would give the high court the power to reverse *Roe*, among other key decisions about human rights, and fulfill the president's campaign promise of criminalizing abortion and punishing women. It would certainly fulfill one of Vice President Mike Pence's most recurring talking points of sending *Roe* back to the "ash heap of history."

Roe v. Wade ranks among perhaps the best known Supreme Court decisions in history, and therefore shouldn't necessitate that much explaining on my end. The question it sought to answer was, at its core, simple: Do women have the right to have safe, legal abortion? In a 7-2 ruling, the high court cited the Constitution's protections of privacy and due process and said yes, women do. The suit had been filed on behalf of Jane Roe of Texas to challenge Texas' ban on elective abortion, and it ultimately resulted in a ruling that granted women the right to abortion until the point of fetal viability—which varies for each woman, or for some women, never even happens—and without undue burden.

Prior to 1973, the year the case was decided, abortion wasn't legal on the federal level, although a handful of states (roughly 13) had, at that point, legalized it. Throughout the 1960s, there were 200,000 to 1.2 million unsafe abortions in the U.S. annually, and thousands of American women died each year as a result. Wealthy women—who also tended to be white women—could afford to travel to states where abortion was safe and legal, and could afford the procedure, making *Roe* slightly less relevant to them. But in slums, low-income communities of color, and immigrant neighborhoods, unsafe abortions were rampant, and common among married women who already had several children and simply couldn't take care of more. Self-induced abortions in the early, mid-20th century weren't what they are, today; today, there is medication abortion, which can be purchased online in some states. Medication abortion differs from dangerous DIY abortions common in pre-*Roe* America and parts of the U.S. with limited abortion access today, because of how safe it is: Serious complications involving medication abortion occur less than 0.25 percent of the time. Nonetheless, access to medication abortion remains far too limited.

In either case, among these marginalized communities prior to *Roe*, there was substantially less access to reliable birth control and sexual health education, which is exactly why birth control activists like Margaret Sanger, the founder of Planned Parenthood, tried to reach out to these communities specifically. Of course, today, advocacy for equal access to abortion and birth control is often spun by the anti-choice movement as targeted "black genocide" or eugenics. But Sanger's work for birth control access was spurred largely by her work as a nurse; she watched emergency rooms and hospitals pile to capacity with women—nearly all of whom were low-income women, women of color, or immigrant women—who had injured themselves trying to end their pregnancies, on a daily basis.

That said, of course, abortion access is and has always been a necessity regardless of one's access to long-term, reliable contraception. According to Guttmacher Institute, a majority—albeit, a slim one—of all abortion patients report having used some form of contraception when they conceived. In other words, to deny women safe, legal abortion is to punish us for the very biological functions of our bodies, for being women (whether already mothers or married women, it doesn't matter), and for having sex.

Abortion bans almost never stop abortion—only safe abortion. The only purpose they serve is to try to force women to give birth and carry to term against our will, to suffer through the indignity and inconvenience of forced pregnancy, or hurt ourselves—sometimes even die—just to make a basic decision about our lives.

Today, the United States maintains the highest maternal mortality rate in the industrialized world, with more pregnancy and birth-related deaths in states where reproductive rights are heavily restricted. In the U.S. and around the world, countries with bans and restrictions on abortions have roughly the same rates of abortion as countries with more liberalized laws, but substantially higher rates of unsafe abortion and maternal deaths. We have seen this reality exacerbated by an executive order signed by President Trump (and first introduced by President Ronald Reagan in the 1980s) in 2017, which stripped global organizations that provide abortion, birth control, or information about abortion of any federal funding. The consequence so far has been increased maternal death rates, dangerous pregnancies among young girls and women, and rates of sexually transmitted infections in poor, majority non-white countries.

The overall decline of the national abortion rate in the U.S. in recent years has largely been attributed to increased access to reliable birth control through the Affordable Care Act's contraception mandate and increasingly liberalized state-by-state laws around birth control access. In contrast, restrictions on abortion have no real bearing on the rate that abortions take place, simply impacting the ratio of safe vs. unsafe abortions.

There are plenty more proof points for why the situation around abortion access remains dire, even with *Roe v. Wade* intact. Following the Tea Party wave of 2010, hundreds of unnecessary, misogyny-driven restrictions on abortion passed in red state legislatures across the country; in fact, more than a quarter of all 1,200 restrictions enacted since *Roe* were passed between 2011 and 2016. Many of these laws, which ranged from bans on abortion at varying stages of pregnancy to medically unnecessary, expensive requirements on clinics resulting in them being forced to shut down en masse, served to shutter access to safe, legal abortion across the country. Specifically, laws requiring abortion clinics to have hospital admitting privileges and hallways that could fit stretchers, among other stringent requirements, are rampant in many states. But, these laws are highly unnecessary considering fewer people go to the emergency room for abortion-related complications than for colonoscopies, most dental operations, and other everyday legal health services.

As of 2014, roughly 90 percent of counties in the U.S. lack an abortion provider. In the year 2015 alone, there were more than 700,000 internet searches for how to complete a DIY abortion around the world; in the United States, there were more than 115,000 searches for how to induce a miscarriage, according to a *New York Times* analysis from 2016.

Since 1976, the Hyde amendment has prohibited federal funding from paying for the costs of elective abortion, an

inherently discriminatory law that has been key to transform-
ing elective abortion from right to privilege. The law has been
justified as a means to respect the "religious freedom" of people
who oppose abortion, all while federal taxpayer dollars continue to pay for foreign wars and military aid that result in the
deaths of born, living human beings. Of course, the hypocrisy
of those who claim to be "pro-life" is ceaseless and well-doc-
umented, manifest in Republican neglect of health care for
children, and the complicity of major "pro-life" politicians and
groups as President Trump ordered migrant children to be torn
from their parents and locked in cages.

In either case, in addition to the Hyde amendment, 32 states
prohibit insurance coverage of elective abortion, and federal
and state-level attempts to defund Planned Parenthood—
which could substantially increase abortion rates by virtue
of increasing unwanted pregnancy rates—are a near weekly
occurrence across the country. What anti-choice lawmakers
don't seem to grasp is that Planned Parenthood and other
women's health organizations already can't allocate federal
funding to pay for elective abortions due to Hyde. This legal
reality is by no means moral, but it certainly makes Republican opponents of Planned Parenthood (even more) wrong in
their demands, just as it, unfortunately, makes abortion even
more stigmatized.

Meanwhile, across the country, thousands of fake women's
health clinics posing as "crisis pregnancy centers" falsely market themselves as abortion providers to lure disproportionately low-income women of color in their doors. They proceed
to peddle disproven lies and misinformation about abortion,
shame and deceive pregnant women, and attack women's right
to make informed, free decisions about their bodies. These

clinics target low-income women who can't afford the costs of ultrasounds, which are required in many states to access abortion care (as of 2018, 26 states require ultrasounds), by offering free ultrasound services. Low-income women often miss work shifts to go to crisis pregnancy centers for health services that ultimately aren't even offered, and as a result, not only waste time they could have spent accessing real health care, but also lose income from missed work.

The myriad barriers to access safe, legal abortion across the country have produced a reality in which, for many Americans, abortion remains legal in name only, with *Roe v. Wade*'s full promise vastly eroded by laws enacted in the post-*Roe* era. Specifically, for poor women, for pregnant victims of rape who are not able to sufficiently prove they were raped to law enforcement or doctors, for immigrant women held hostage in detainment centers, and for the 58 percent of American women who live in states recognized by Guttmacher Institute as "hostile to abortion rights," abortion is a right in name only. Cost, geography, and gendered animus from lawmakers have isolated abortion from all other safe, legal medical services for decades despite how *Roe* technically bans laws that pose undue burdens on abortion access, and this reality has been exacerbated in recent years with the rise of the Tea Party.

But of course, it's more than underhanded, malicious laws that are obstructing abortion access and endangering women's lives. There also exists a dangerous, overarching culture of violence and stigma around reproductive rights. In 2015 alone, three abortion providers were murdered while nine faced documented attempted murders. In the first half of 2016, 34.2 percent of abortion providers in the U.S. reported being subjected to "severe violence or threats of violence," compared with the previous high, which was 24 percent of providers experiencing violence or threats over the course of 1995, according to the Feminist Majority Foundation. This frightening uptick in violence was no coincidence: In the summer of 2015, anti-abortion extremists performed a sting operation to illegally obtain video of Planned Parenthood workers purportedly "selling baby parts"—or, in other words, seeking reimbursement for providing fetal tissue for medical research. The "selling baby parts" line almost immediately became a rallying cry within the anti-choice movement, and fueled increasingly aggressive, morbid rhetoric from Republican politicians with vast platforms and cultural influence. Within months, a Colorado man with a history of domestic violence styled himself as a "warrior for the babies," held a local Planned Parenthood clinic hostage, and wound up killing three in a shooting spree.

In 2018, conservative commentator and former *Atlantic* columnist Kevin Williamson said women who have abortions—or, in other words, a quarter of all women—should be subjected to the death penalty by hanging. Former Idaho state representative and then-candidate for Idaho lieutenant governor Bob Nonini similarly and enthusiastically cheered for the death penalty for those who have abortions, within weeks of Williamson's comments. While some on the right attempted to distance themselves from these policy proposals, for years, the anti-choice movement has failed to reconcile its rhetoric that says abortion is murder and kills "babies" with how they believe women who have abortions should be treated, if abortion is, indeed, murder.

While Vice President Mike Pence served as Governor of Indiana, the state saw multiple women—and notably women of color—jailed for the outcomes of their pregnancies; in 2016, Donald Trump said explicitly that "there has to be some form of punishment" for women who have abortions. If abortion were criminalized, women would almost certainly be investigated and perhaps even jailed for miscarriages, especially in light of how common it is for anti-choice politicians to conflate abortion and miscarriage. In 2018, a Walgreens pharmacist in Arizona who opposed abortion cited religious freedom to deny a woman who had experienced a miscarriage her prescribed abortion medication.

The end of *Roe v. Wade* is undeniably about abortion—but abortion itself isn't just about abortion. In a country without *Roe* and its full protections, women would be subjected to surveillance and punishment for pregnancy itself.

Just as stigma around abortion has resulted in laws that treat it differently from all other equally legal, equally safe medical services, stigma has also created a culture of targeted harassment and violence against women who have abortions, and doctors who provide abortion services. From anti-choice protesters who pave the sidewalks of women's health clinics, to arsonists and murderers who inflict terror on abortion providers regularly, to commentators and politicians cheering for the death penalty for women and doctors, the violence that pervades the movement for reproductive justice is a reflection of just how dangerous abortion stigma is.

Stigma is the reason Planned Parenthood is forced to advertise that abortion constitutes just 3 percent of all services that it provides, and remind us that none of the federal funding it receives pays for elective abortion. Stigma is the reason women's health providers that offer abortion care must play defense, rather than proactively demand an end to discriminatory laws that effectively ban abortion based on economic status, and unapologetically market the abortion care they provide. Stigma is the reason pro-choice politicians and advocates feel pressured to signal their support for reproductive rights without saying the word "abortion," and all too often neglect the independent abortion clinics across the country that lack the funding, donors, and name recognition of Planned Parenthood, but provide the majority of all abortions in the U.S.

Even in a country where *Roe v. Wade* is supposedly the law of the land, women continue to navigate ideologically motivated laws and violence, which collude to make abortion inaccessible for some, and difficult to access for others, while those who have abortions or advocate for abortion rights are told to feel ashamed.

That said, I would suggest trying to imagine, then, what the U.S. without *Roe* would look like, but the truth is, we don't have to imagine: thousands of women died from unsafe abortions every year before 1973. Today, in states with more abortion restrictions, internet searches for how to induce miscarriages spike and women pay outrageously expensive costs to travel to states where abortion is more accessible. In the days and weeks following Kennedy's announcement, women's magazines as well as the *New York Times, Washington Post,* and other major newspapers published the stories of women who had had unsafe abortions by the dozen—stories of women asking boyfriends to punch them in the stomach, consuming laundry detergent or rat poison, trying to get into intentional car accidents, and, yes, reaching for wire hangers.

The circumstances in the U.S. even with *Roe* in place are subpar to put it gently. A 2017 study by the Population Reference Bureau found millennial women's living standards are worse than their mothers' due to how dramatically abortion access has shuttered in the decades following an era of relatively liberalized abortion laws in the late 20th century.

And yet, that said, it could and likely will get so much worse if we continue down this road, and reverse *Roe* and its full promise altogether.

IT SHOULD GO WITHOUT SAYING, but *Roe v. Wade* remains important despite how systemic legal attacks on the precedent have obstructed its ability to serve as a cure-all solution for reproductive rights. *Roe* provides the legal basis for pro-choice lawyers to argue against laws that place undue burden on women seeking abortion care. It serves as a powerful statement about who we are as a country to the rest of the world, a statement that says American women are allowed to be proactive players in their lives and destinies. It's a statement that women are human beings, because bodily autonomy *is* personhood, and if this is taken away by abortion bans and restrictions, women are effectively stripped of their personhood as a result. To be clear, it is impossible—simply impossible—to confer personhood on fertilized eggs and unviable fetuses, without first stripping women of that personhood, and relegating all women to mere state incubators.

Perhaps, wittingly or not, Oklahoma state Rep. Justin Humphrey (a Republican, if you can believe) put it best—or at least made this sentiment clearest—in 2017, when he said of women: "I understand that they feel like that is their body. I feel like it is a separate—what I call them is, is you're a 'host.'" Humphrey had been trying to sell his bill that would require women seeking abortions to have the written consent of the fetus' father.

Attorney General Jeff Sessions' arguments about abortion have raised similar existential questions about the humanity of women—most notably, when his lawyers argued that the Trump administration had the right to hold detained undocumented minors seeking abortion hostage, and force girls as young as 12 to carry to term, even if they were impregnated by rape. His argument had been that citizens and non-citizens inherently have different rights, and, specifically, that non-citizens lack human rights in the United States. Brett Kavanaugh, President Trump's nominee to succeed Justice Kennedy, affirmed this rationale, arguing while on the D.C. Circuit Court that imprisoning pregnant immigrant women and girls in detainment centers somehow did not pose an "undue burden" on abortion access.

Roe matters, and the country, as well as the whole world, would be worse off without it. The threat that its reversal poses to women is real—and the threat that *Roe*'s existence will face under a conservative-majority Supreme Court is real, too.

———

IN THE MOMENTS AND DAYS and weeks following Anthony Kennedy's retirement, chaos and fear weren't exclusively contained within the office I worked at. Uncertainty, terror, and outrage reigned across the country, and certainly on social media. And yet, anxiety over the future of women's health, safety, and rights was, predictably enough, contained mostly among women.

Men supported the confirmation of Kavanaugh at a rate of 47 percent compared to 28 percent of women, according to polling from the summer of 2018 that also revealed Kavanaugh was the least popular Supreme Court Justice nominee in modern U.S. history. (Coincidentally, American men didn't face the prospect of being forced to give birth pending Kavanaugh's confirmation.) Another telling poll revealed that around three weeks after Trump nominated Kavanaugh, the vast majority of voters by a margin of 62 to 27 percent believed that it was "not likely" that *Roe v. Wade* would be overturned in the next few years.

But of course, here is the reality of just how precarious *Roe v. Wade* is as of 2018: Within just two years of Trump's presidency, he has already appointed more than an eighth of all circuit court judges across the country. And as state legislatures in red states, purple states, and even some blue states pump out everything from bans on safe abortion in the second trimester, to underhanded hospital admitting privilege requirements that shut down clinics en masse, abortion laws constantly result in lawsuits, often working their ways up to circuit courts and beyond.

The surge of extremist, blatantly unconstitutional anti-abortion laws being proposed in state legislatures, and sometimes passed and subsequently challenged in court, are part of a very deliberate right-wing, anti-choice strategy. Anti-choice lawmakers know their most extreme laws, if passed, will inevitably be challenged in court—that's their goal. They're essentially playing a game of throwing spaghetti at the wall and seeing what will stick, and by stick, I mean end up being passed all the way to the Supreme Court. Upon solidifying a conservative, anti-abortion majority on the Supreme Court bench, conservatives' end-game is to ensure any decision on cases about abortion will result in *Roe* being either reversed or dramatically scaled back. In the absence of *Roe*, a Republican Congress could subsequently pass legislation to criminalize abortion, or state legislatures and governors' offices could just as easily do the job in their respective states. Around 20 states as of 2018 maintain "trigger laws," or laws that would immediately make abortion illegal the moment *Roe* is reversed.

In 2018 alone, Iowa passed and briefly enacted a fetal heartbeat abortion ban, which would ban abortion before most women even know they're pregnant; Arkansas passed a ban on medication abortion; and Mississippi passed a ban on abortion at or after 15 weeks—which can also be before some women know they're pregnant. Each of these laws wound up in circuit courts, and with enough anti-choice judges in courts across the country, any abortion law could easily, eventually be filed to the Supreme Court; if accepted by the Supreme Court, an anti-choice majority could either uphold these laws, or even see fit to strike the precedent of *Roe* altogether.

The confirmation of so many of Trump's radically unqualified, far-right extremist judges has been enabled by a Republican-majority Senate, which also has the power to confirm Trump's even more dangerous Supreme Court nominees. The election of Donald Trump was a coup from day one: The consolidation of the Republican Party's power across all branches of government as well as the majority of state legislatures meant the fulfillment of the ultimate goal of Republicans' decades-long War on Women. The retirement of Anthony Kennedy, the last Supreme Court justice who would protect *Roe*, effectively spelled the War on Women's end-game.

And yet, even as advocacy groups like NARAL Pro-Choice America, Planned Parenthood and the National Network of Abortion Funds began actively preparing to exist and offer care and support in a post-*Roe* nation; even as state governors in Massachusetts, Oregon, New York, and other states moved to proactively encode abortion rights into state law in anticipation of impending realities; and even as, across the aisle, anti-choice organizers in states like West Virginia and Alabama launched ballot initiatives to end abortion rights, men of all political ideologies were armed and ready with the words "calm down."

At first, it was centrist, perhaps even liberal-leaning men like journalist Brian Stelter, who took to Twitter within hours of Kennedy's announcement to respond to a woman writer who drew a comparison between the dystopic story and Hulu drama, *The Handmaid's Tale,* and the future of the United States: "We are not 'a few steps from 'The Handmaids Tale,'" he wrote, adding, "I don't think this kind of fear-mongering helps anybody."

Women's responses to his tweet were almost immediate.

Shannon Coulter, founder of the "Grab Your Wallet" initiative to boycott the Trumps, replied: "My dude, I respect you in general, but we SO do not want or need you trying to tell us when to make Handmaid's Tale comparisons. You frankly have no idea what women go through in terms of their bodies and reproductive rights in this country, so just put a big ol' cork in it."

Journalist Erin Biba pointed out the problematic nature of regarding marginalized people's expressions and characterizations of their oppression, rather than their oppression itself, as the problem: "When you don't like how people are characterizing their own oppression it's probably less effective to argue with the characterization then it would be to, say, just try to get into the fight to stop the oppression," she wrote.

Allure writer Hayley Macmillen chimed in on Twitter, too, although not directly in response to Stelter's tweet: "If your first instinct is to insist things aren't 'that bad' or to try to talk others out of their anger and fear, please ask yourself why you feel the need to minimize serious pain and real threats to safety, health, and rights. Then ask why you're not doing something instead," she wrote.

Former Obama staffer Ronald Klain stood up for women, writing in a tweet, "Anyone who tells you that *Roe v. Wade* is 'not really at risk' doesn't know what they are talking about. Anyone who votes for Trump's nominee is voting to overturn *Roe*. Period."

Of course, those with beliefs similar to Stelter's continued to share. From a *Wall Street Journal* editorial board slamming the possibility of *Roe*'s reversal as left-wing farce, to a *Washington Post* op-ed quite literally titled, "Calm down. *Roe v. Wade* isn't going anywhere," instead of pushing back on the political forces conspiring before our eyes to steal women's livelihood and autonomy, men and media figures of all political ideologies seemed to regard the real problem as women's fear and expression of that fear.

Comedian Samantha Bee summed up the situation aptly in a *Full Frontal* segment when she said, "All Republicans have done for years is rail against abortion, and now suddenly we're hysterical for taking them at their word?"

Even among the right-wing media outlets and politicians who had once so gleefully called abortion murder and demanded the immediate reversal of *Roe*, just to subject women to the indignity of fearmongering and hysteria accusations, they momentarily reversed course and argued that nothing about Brett Kavanaugh's "moderate" record suggested he would vote against *Roe*, that feminists were just overreacting as per the usual. Outlets like The Federalist, Townhall, and others made it rain with op-eds claiming that anyone afraid for the future of *Roe* was delusional or exaggerating.

Subsequently, in a report called, "Don't buy right-wing media's gaslighting: Brett Kavanaugh is a threat to abortion access," Media Matters for America documented the dozens of instances of conservative media and politicians mocking women's fears about the future of *Roe*, juxtaposed with years of right-wing politicians quite literally identifying the end of legal abortion as their goal.

It wasn't just Mike Pence who had promised to drag the country back to the days before *Roe*: State legislatures across the country have been proposing bans on all abortion for years; banning safe, legal abortion was listed on the 2016 Republican Party platform, and anti-choice ideology has almost become a litmus test for the Party at large.

In other words, fear about how Kavanaugh or any Trump judicial nominee would vote on abortion was wholly rooted in reality. In addition to advocating that the Trump administration had the right to imprison undocumented, pregnant minors, Kavanaugh had also praised the dissent in *Roe v. Wade* in a very public speech less than a year before being nominated. He had ruled in favor of insurers and employers' rights to discriminate against women and deny women birth control coverage on the basis of "religious freedom," ignoring how denying women health care for failing to conform to Christian values violates women's right to religious freedom.

From the aforementioned 62 percent of surveyed voters who denied *Roe* was at risk, from those who ignored or belittled the women and policy experts who had thoroughly proven how Kavanaugh could and would serve as the fifth vote to end *Roe* as early as next summer, what we encountered was gaslighting, plain and simple. The dominant attitudes surrounding the Kennedy vacancy and nomination of Kavanaugh reflected an infuriatingly stubborn refusal to believe women, even when our lives quite literally depended on our concerns being believed. We were not only disbelieved, but shamed, humiliated, and called liars. Perhaps many of that 62 percent constituency were, indeed, ignorant to the reality of what was at stake. But the right wing's refusal to own up to its own self-identified agenda of ending legal abortion was part of its game: to portray women as hysterical before quite literally killing us.

We should have been listening to women—women with stories of wire hangers and rat poison, women who have lived our collective, universal nightmare firsthand—rather than male commentators who lacked any real stakes in what was happening. But is it any surprise that we didn't? We don't take women seriously, nor do we believe them—we never have. The cruel, compassionless cynicism of a society that requires women to jump through hoops to prove our pain and be listened to and validated certainly isn't new. This cynicism has degraded women for generations, resulting in men persistently claiming to know more about the realities we face despite never experiencing what we have.

I watched as women and feminist writers, activists, and allies around me became increasingly exasperated, tired of explaining, tired of justifying their fear. In addition to facing this nearly unprecedented threat, they also faced the burden of being forced to prove the threat even existed, to try to convince people to actually care.

Overturning *Roe* and reversing decades of progress—albeit often slow progress—had been a campaign promise of the Trump-Pence administration, and Kennedy's retirement and Kavanaugh's nomination served as the vehicle through which this was possible. Anyone who has chastised women for "fearmongering" about the future of our reproductive rights is either ignorant to this reality, or simply gaslighting us. And this includes not only Brian Stelter and the *Wall Street Journal* editorial board—to an extent, it also includes House Minority Leader Nancy Pelosi, who in 2017 claimed that abortion rights were a "fading issue"; Vice President Joe Biden, who has claimed that abortion rights are a "settled" issue; and Bernie Sanders and his cautions against focusing on "identity politics" and the "social issue" of abortion.

Abortion rights are and have always been our livelihood. They have never been secure, they have never been settled, and the threat they face today is unprecedented in modern history. It's true that almost 50 years after *Roe*, we shouldn't be here—abortion *should* be a fading issue, it *should* be settled, it *should* be so economically accessible to all women that we could dismiss it with ease as a "social issue." But that's not where we are. And if you spent even a moment listening to women who have had abortions, to people whose livelihoods rest on this fundamental human right, you'd know this.

The majority of Americans do not believe *Roe v. Wade* is really in danger. They do not believe that we are on the brink of living in a country where abortion is criminal, and women and doctors are punished. But here is another reality: The majority of Americans also support *Roe*. More than seven in 10 Americans support abortion rights, and that number increases among younger Americans. In the hypothetical and not unlikely absence of *Roe*, we who comprise this majority will show up; we will raise money for abortion funds, we will drive women to states where abortion is legal and provide them with lodging. We will protest every day; we will call our representatives on every level of government, we will be relentless.

The fight for women's rights has never been a straight line. It has always been a long arc, and one paved with loss and challenge, struggle and death. And it has never been shut down or ended by any one, single outcome; it has never been shut down or ended by the will of one man, or five men in black robes.

The right's attempt to gaslight us into believing that abortion rights are safe, and that we're crazy if we believe there is any real threat to *Roe,* is misogyny, yes—but it's also strategy. They know we are the majority and the future of this country. They know if we are aware of the existential threat we face, and subsequently show up and fight, that we can and will win the War on Women.

So that's exactly what we have to do, every single day, no matter what happens, no matter how many battles we lose. We have to treat reproductive rights as a fight that is not contingent on any single result; we have to treat reproductive rights as the fight of and for our lives. For many women and people, that's exactly what they are.

DON'T GET ME WRONG—plenty of other issues are at stake with a new conservative justice on the Supreme Court. Of course, I know it's not just abortion and birth control, although speaking pragmatically, all of the other rights on the chopping block with Brett Kavanaugh's appointment are, in themselves, women's rights: Women's rights *are* labor rights, health care rights, voting rights, immigration rights; women exist everywhere and are affected often disproportionately by any oppressive policy you could name.

But the fear that I and so many women feel about abortion,

in particular, stems from what we have seen throughout history: Women's rights are the first to go.

Even within the Democratic Party, with mounting calls from Party leadership to embrace "pro-life" Democrats, which would purportedly draw electoral wins in red states, we are seeing women's rights relegated to collateral damage for some imagined utilitarian outcome. I hope I've made clear enough, based alone on how many women die as a result of bans on abortion, that abortion rights are not an issue upon which we can safely compromise—not without killing women, ruining their lives, and ultimately degrading them to second-class citizens.

To be clear, there are other frankly more effective ways to win elections in red states, such as fighting voter suppression and proactively reaching out to communities that are historically excluded from electoral processes, as we saw in the very pro-choice Doug Jones' 2017 victory over the very anti-choice Roy Moore in Alabama. Democratic Party leadership's decision to say that abortion rights are not important, and fundraise for and support anti-choice Democrats is an unnecessary, terrifying, and vastly harmful choice.

I'm certain that when it comes to the Supreme Court, we'll encounter something not so different. For many voters on the right, voters who may have been disgusted or uncomfortable with nearly everything Trump said or did, abortion rights and the immediate necessity of ending abortion rights were all they saw in the 2016 election, much like a sort of twisted, misogynistic tunnel vision. It's hard to say how many, but certainly many voted for Trump solely because of abortion, solely because of the high chance that three to four Supreme Court justices could die or retire between 2017 and 2021, giving the next president the key to whether women across the country will live or die.

Of course abortion will be the first to go if Trump secures an anti-choice majority on the court, and I don't just mean that because as of 2018, the cases that could end *Roe* are already in the courts. I say that because it is a universal, generational truth. So don't ever believe anyone who tells you we are worried over nothing, don't ever listen to anyone who tells us to calm down. We have spent our lives on the chopping block waiting for this day, old women, young women, and the generations of women before and after us. The only way the right could ever stop us from fighting for our rights and lives is through gaslighting us into believing there is no fight to be had, that everything is just fine. But we know. We know and are ready for what's coming because all of our lives have prepared us for this.

And so, that said, here's what we're going to do: Fight. Call our senators, rally outside their offices, march the streets, run for office, fundraise for abortion funds, drive women across state lines to have abortions, care for women's children when they go out of town to have their abortions, vote for lawmakers up and down the ballots who will protect abortion rights, protest the nominations of judges who would hurt abortion rights, collect signatures for ballot measures to protect abortion rights, and so on, and so forth, every day for the rest of our lives.

We do not need more commentary about abortion and our human rights—we've heard plenty of it, all our lives, every "calm down," every "it's not that bad," every accusation that we're exaggerating our pain. We always knew this was the direction we were heading, we always knew we'd receive no help from the men who never saw or were willing to concede this ultimate threat to our bodily autonomy. But now we're here— and now, we're ready.

THE "PRO-LIFE" MOVEMENT:
THE FIRST FAKE NEWS

Gaslighting isn't always just mind games and condescending, misogyny-laced cynicism that tells women to question our most fundamental experiences and opinions. It's also often blatant, outright lies.

We hear the term "fake news" a lot these days, often in reference to media outlets directly quoting President Trump and other Republicans, and in doing so, shining a light on the racism, misogyny, and bigotry the Party has for years tried to hide. Quite famously in the summer of 2018, Republican Congressman and Freedom Caucus member Rep. Jim Jordan bemoaned CNN's investigation of accusations that he enabled and covered sexual abuse at Ohio State University, calling the news outlet's interviews with hundreds of people he'd worked with "fake news." Many were quick to point out the irony of how, in decrying "fake news," Jordan had inadvertently given a definition of responsible, real journalism.

In an era in which dog whistles have become barks, it's impossible to hide most things, and certainly impossible to hide the cruelty and hatred that belie nearly every major, impactful policy decision by this presidential administration and the

Republican-controlled Congress with which it colludes. But there is, certainly, real "fake news"—most of it coming from the president and his sympathizers, themselves, as they peddle out disproven, objective lies day after day, and pretend that those who question these lies are the liars.

And, of course, there's also the "pro-life" movement.

Long before the term "fake news" existed, there were people pretending a movement to control, shame, and punish women was really about children and families, pushing campaign after campaign of pseudoscience and loaded vocabulary, and attempting to shut down accusations of misogyny and the voices of real women with fearmongering photos of bloodied fetuses.

Long before "fake news" became the motto of Trump and his base, there were lawmakers across the country overlooking every credible study proving the safety of abortion and passing restrictive laws by pushing out lie after lie that abortion hurts women.

In California beginning in 2016, state legislators began considering Senate Bill 320, a bill that would fund and require public universities to carry medication abortion in campus health centers. The bill acknowledged how travel costs; being forced to miss class, work, and internships for off-campus abortions; and spending hours researching where and how to access abortion perpetuated gender inequality on college campuses, which could have the effect of limiting college women's opportunities and creating gender achievement gaps. S.B. 320 not only offered but also funded a solution to this prevalent struggle that didn't even involve taxpayer spending, due to private donors and fundraising efforts by leading state women's organizations.

Pushback against the bill, even in a state with a climate around abortion as liberal as California's, thus focused solely on the safety of abortion, since S.B. 320 explicitly did not involve public funding. Forget that medication abortion causes major complications less than 0.25 percent of the time, and how one in four women will have an abortion by age 45, regardless of whether they have access to safe abortion—the campaign against S.B. 320, as anti-abortion campaigns so often are, was unabashed lies and deceit.

The "pro-life" movement has never been about children but hurting women—often first by maligning women who have abortions. Fifty-nine percent of women who have abortions are already mothers, while 46 percent are living with a long-term partner when they have their abortion. Additionally, the majority of all abortion patients report having used some form of contraception when they conceived. To limit and oppose abortion is sexual policing, punishing women for the very nature of their bodies and biology plain and simple, no matter what spin "pro-lifers" may offer. As Slate's Christia Cauterucci put it in a July 2018 essay:

> "Denying women abortions isn't, as anti-abortion advocates often claim, just about saving the lives of unborn children. It's also about imposing a moral judgment on women for having sex. Pro-lifers tend to frame childbirth as a consequence any sexually active single woman should be ready to assume. The phrase *abortion on demand*, a popular encapsulation of the presumed position of the pro-choice set, suggests that certain women, by virtue of their reasons or circumstances, deserve abortions more than others. Many, but not all, right-wing politicians make room within their anti-abortion frameworks for exceptions in cases of rape and incest.

"Their thinking goes something like this: A woman who was raped had no ability to prevent her pregnancy. Every other woman who gets pregnant bears the responsibility for doing so, and their bodies must suffer for failing to accept that responsibility, even if it means bringing a child into a family who is unable or unwilling to properly care for it."

In no uncertain terms, the "pro-life" movement is fraud—terrifying, fundamentalist fraud that has enabled and empowered just about every awful abortion law that's ever passed, every threat and act of violence against abortion providers and women who have abortions. And that fraud starts with the movement's name. It seems redundant to say at this point, what with all the deaths of women that anti-abortion laws and unsafe abortions have caused over the course of human history, but the movement against abortion has no real concern for life, nor for quality of life for women and children.

Fetuses and fertilized eggs are not children, and this statement of fact is not rooted in political sentiment, or ideology, or anything other than objective science. In a similar vein, there is also no conclusive science to suggest fetuses feel pain the same way that we, born, living humans do.

The fact that abortion opponents do not care about children is similarly rooted in evidence, not politics. It's rooted in their collusion with the Republican Party, which neglected to renew the Children's Health Insurance Program through which some nine million low-income children access life-saving health care, for almost a full year between 2017 and 2018. The Party repeatedly used this program as leverage to threaten and cajole Congressional Democrats to yield on the rights of immigrant children. And while some self-identified pro-lifers, including many members of organized religion and Republican higher-ups, opposed the Trump administration's family separation policy in 2018, anti-choice groups like Susan B. Anthony's List either declined to take a stance on family separation, or pivoted with the weak, crassly hypocritical statement that abortion—a health service that enables many low-income families to survive—was the "real" family separation.

Whether or not groups like this speak for all members of the anti-choice movement, it matters that as a unit, a movement claiming to love children and families was not able to provide a unified, unequivocal condemnation of a policy of abject child abuse. It matters because it exposed their true colors, and real goals: controlling women—and valuing white children and families over brown children and families.

Whereas evidence that the "pro-life" movement has any genuine intention to support born, living children and families is virtually nonexistent, evidence substantiating its hostility to children and families is frankly boundless. It's in the deafening silence of "pro-life" lawmakers and groups whenever yet another young, unarmed black man is shot to death by police; it's in "pro-life" lawmakers' cruel votes in favor of anti-immigration laws and systems of mass incarceration that have torn families of color apart for decades. It's in tireless "pro-life" votes against common-sense gun control laws, even amid school shooting after school shooting aided by legally purchased firearms. It's in vehement opposition to programs for sexual health education and birth control access, yielding shameful teen pregnancy and STI rates that can disrupt the whole trajectory of young people's lives. And perhaps above all, it's in their refusal to acknowledge how abortion bans have only ever prevented safe abortion, while driving up rates of death and injury caused by unsafe abortions and pregnancy-related maternal deaths in the U.S.

Broadly speaking, their disdain for life is evident in the right's utter disregard for any programs that offer meaningful, dignified living standards to born, living children and adults who aren't wealthy or white. And let's just say that if your name, itself, is a transparent, easily discredited lie, we can't really expect things to get better from there. The "pro-life" movement isn't just a war on women—it's also a war on truth.

IN 2015, A RIGHT-WING GROUP illegally recorded and proceeded to edit and manipulate video footage from a sting operation at a Planned Parenthood clinic. Two years later, the activists responsible were charged with 15 felonies, which should give you a rough idea about the circumstances in which the video was recorded, produced and released. But despite this accountability, the videos and the "selling baby parts" rallying cry that the videos yielded have irrevocably poisoned the dialogue and greater political environment around abortion rights, perhaps for generations.

The videos take a conversation about compensation for providing fetal tissue for medical research grossly out of context, and not so coincidentally preceded a trend of violence targeting abortion clinics across the country. Following the release of the videos, arson, bomb threats, murder threats, and even completed murders ravaged clinics, and rather than launch an investigation of the forces threatening providers of a legal, safe medical service, Congress allocated more than $1.6 million to investigating whether Planned Parenthood "sells baby parts" that same year.

As right-wing, anti-choice narratives so often do, the myth of Planned Parenthood selling baby parts radically and dangerously oversimplifies reality—and, specifically, what donating fetal tissue actually means. Historically, the Republican Party has voted in favor of allowing tissue from aborted fetuses to be donated for medical research. In the 20th century, aborted fetal tissue helped yield a life-saving cure for polio. The outrage directed at Planned Parenthood for this decades-old tradition which has saved unquantifiable lives is explicitly rooted in situational context—that is, the stigma around abortion and female bodily autonomy.

Nonetheless, the fake news videos had real—and terrifying—consequences. Months after the videos were released, Robert Dear of Colorado attacked a Planned Parenthood in his state, killing three and injuring many with a legally purchased firearm. He styled himself as a "warrior for the babies," which should make his motives perfectly clear.

And, of course, all while that was happening, a crowded field of Republican presidential candidates capitalized on every opportunity to attack Planned Parenthood, and bring up the "baby parts" videos. Spewing fake news of epic proportions, then-Republican candidate Carly Fiorina described footage of "a fully formed fetus on the table, its heart beating, its legs kicking, while someone [said], 'We have to keep it alive to harvest its brain,'" at a presidential debate. No one really knows what video she was talking about (perhaps, and this is just a wild guess here, it doesn't exist); but the lie was rooted in the videos released that summer. The videos proved to be fodder for a base of extremists that has never cared much for facts and has always seized on quite literally any opportunity to use shock factor and emotional manipulation to demonize abortion.

Later that year and in the years that have followed, Congress has attempted on multiple occasions to defund Planned Parenthood, ignoring how 1) no federal funding pays for abortion services (But should it? Yes.), 2) abortion constitutes 3 percent of the organization's services (Would it matter if abortion comprised 90 or 100 percent of their services? No.), and 3) how compensation for producing and providing fetal tissue for medical research is fundamentally not the same thing as "selling baby parts." Funding attacks on Planned Parenthood have been met with success in states like Indiana, Ohio, Texas, and others, and in states where Planned Parenthood lost some or all funding, clinics were forced to shut down as a result. In at least one documented case of a county in Indiana, the proliferation of HIV and other STIs ensued as a direct consequence.

In other states, the anti-choice movement's opposition to fetal tissue research has also been a boon to anti-vaxxers. Specifically, in Michigan, Senate Bill 1055, which the state Senate moved forward for consideration in 2018, would require that parents and children receive information about how vaccines are cultivated from aborted fetal tissue to enable "informed consent."

The threat that the anti-choice movement's propaganda poses, as well as its range of consequences which include violence, disastrous legislation, and public health crises, is real, too.

A COUPLE DAYS BEFORE Justice Anthony Kennedy announced his retirement from the Supreme Court, he voted in line with the all-male majority in the 5-4 decision, *NIFLA v. Becerra*. *NIFLA*, which stands for National Institute of Family and Life Advocates, was a lawsuit filed on behalf of anti-abortion "crisis pregnancy centers" in California, in response to a state law that required these "clinics" to disclose that they were not licensed medical providers, inform women who enter that they did not offer abortion services, and tell women they have the option to have abortions, elsewhere. In its lawsuit, *NIFLA* argued that the Reproductive FACT (Freedom, Accountability, Comprehensive Care, and Transparency) Act was a violation of anti-choice clinics' First Amendment rights and constituted "compelled speech."

While the Supreme Court's three women—joined by Justice Stephen Breyer—recognized the purposeful deception of crisis pregnancy centers, exacerbated by the internet and potent enabling by Google's search engine, Kennedy and four other men ruled in favor of *NIFLA*, essentially giving fake clinics a free pass to continue their false advertising campaigns, and targeting of low-income women and women of color who are left without meaningful options.

Of course, some have argued that this ruling may not achieve all that abortion opponents intended. A ruling against "compelled speech," after all, could and should work both ways. As of 2018, Arkansas, Arizona, and South Dakota have passed laws requiring doctors who prescribe medication abortion to tell women about the "abortion reversal" option, a widely discredited method to supposedly negate the effects of medication abortion by consuming large amounts of progesterone after taking the first of two abortion pills. Not only do experts say this is dangerous, but additionally, consuming progesterone after taking the first pill has roughly the same rate of negating the abortion as taking the first pill and not taking the second pill within six to 48 hours.

These laws, which range from emotionally abusive to

physically dangerous, have existed for years, and the Supreme Court's decision to allow fake clinics to lie to and deny women the right to make educated decisions about their bodies, marks a distinct, infuriating double standard. The only possible good that could emerge from the ruling is that it could potentially apply to existing mandatory counseling laws in some states. But many of these laws have existed for so long, unlike the relatively new California Reproductive FACT Act enacted in 2016, that using the *NIFLA* decision to overturn them would certainly be an uphill battle. And in either case, it may be difficult to persuade anyone that a ruling transparently meant to protect anti-choice clinics and throw women under the bus could actually be about protecting women.

In no uncertain terms, the *NIFLA* case was a story of women coming forward, raising their voices, and declaring unilaterally that they were being lied to and preyed upon, that this mass, coordinated system of deceit had the capacity to ruin lives and rob the nation's most vulnerable of meaningful autonomy. The decision made by five men should speak volumes about the reality of how women's voices and testimonies are treated in this country.

Thousands of these clinics exist across the country, in some states often outnumbering real, licensed clinics that offer women health care, factual information, and meaningful options. Where a massive wave of anti-abortion laws have shuttered access to real clinics and abortion providers across the country, fake women's health clinics continue to thrive, bankrolled by anti-choice billionaires concentrated in the state of Texas, and often benefiting from taxpayer funding. Meanwhile, as of 2018, seven states have just one abortion clinic to serve millions of women of reproductive age, and roughly 90 percent of counties across the country lack an abortion provider.

There are over 27 abortion deserts, or regions where women must travel more than 100 miles to access abortion, in the United States as of 2018. In Illinois, there is one abortion clinic for every 120,135 women of reproductive age, and in Wisconsin, there is one clinic for every 423,590 women.

Notably, states where abortion is less accessible also tend to have more restrictions on abortion, such as policies that mandate ultrasounds and waiting periods, among other requirements that range from inconvenient and unnecessary to dangerous and jarringly classist. Women in these regions often incur substantial fees from traveling to have a procedure that, in about 32 states, cannot be covered by health insurance with few exceptions. Low-income women, who are more likely to experience unwanted pregnancy because of their limited access to long-term, reliable birth control, are often lured into fake clinics by the promise of free ultrasounds if they live in states where women are required to have ultrasounds in order to access abortion care.

Upon entering the "clinic," they're subsequently told that abortion can cause cancer (false); depression (false—actually, being denied abortion services is directly correlated with depression); infertility (false—although unsafe abortions, often caused by bans and restrictions on legal abortion, can cause this); and a whole range of other lies about personhood. All of this infringes on women's right to informed choice, to abortion access without undue burden, and strips women of—what was that term Michigan anti-vaxxers used?—informed consent.

States that require ultrasounds also often require that ultrasounds be performed at the same clinic in which the pregnant woman has the abortion, and often mandate a waiting period after the ultrasound. To that end, fake clinics have the potential to drastically delay women from accessing abortion care; for low-income women who live in abortion deserts, or do not receive paid time off and have to miss work to travel for their abortion, these clinics prey on their poverty, luring them in with free ultrasound offers, and proceed to exacerbate their poverty by forcing them to miss days of work at a time.

In states where women must travel substantial distances to have abortions, this also places low-income mothers in a difficult position without access to affordable childcare. Fifty-nine percent of women who have abortions are already mothers. Fake clinics often merely stretch out the process of having an abortion, ensnaring poor women with promises of much-needed savings, and subjecting them to relentless, manipulative, and time-consuming lecturing instead As a result, women seeking abortions incur more costs they simply can't afford—especially when those costs also include child care, travel, and lost income from missing work.

The *NIFLA* decision marked a direct attack on poor, pregnant women, and insisted that the right of religious people to lie to and deceive poor women matters more than unbiased health care for women. Perhaps it's early to say what *NIFLA*'s generational consequences will be. But to be sure, the decision marked a roadblock for crucial progress that has been underway for the past few years and enables the continuation of a status quo of dishonesty, manipulation, and predation of women.

Of course, enforcement of Supreme Court decisions is often another story. *Whole Women's Health v. Hellerstedt* in 2016 should have put an end to TRAP laws, or the targeted regulation of abortion providers through laws that are justified with feigned concern over women's safety.

And yet, it's been years since *Whole Women's Health* was decided, and medically unnecessary laws that shut down clinics persist across the country. In Texas, between 2013 and 2016, 22 of the state's 41 abortion clinics shut down within three years after the state first passed the TRAP law, House Bill 2.

The *NIFLA* decision marked a direct attack on poor, pregnant women, and insisted that the right of religious people to lie and deceive matters more than unbiased health care for women.

Long before the term became popularized, "fake news" and the systemic targeting of low-income women with both lies and the withholding of the truth have allowed the "pro-life" movement to subsist and hold progress hostage in an evolving country for generations.

———

FAKE CLINICS ARE PROACTIVE about pushing lies, but their silence about women's option to have an abortion and refusal to admit that they don't offer real health care is equally exploitative, equally immoral, equally damaging. Silence often is all of those things—exploitative, immoral, damaging—especially in the context of women's health, safety, and autonomy.

Within days of his inauguration, Donald Trump signed an executive order to reinstate the Mexico City policy, first established by President Ronald Reagan. The law is widely known as the global gag rule, as it withholds funding from any global organization that offers abortion and contraception services, or even education about these options. In developing and often majority non-white countries, this education has been life-saving. It's taught adolescent girls, many of whom wind up forced into child marriages, how to prevent dangerous pregnancies. Even in less extreme cases, unintended pregnancies, which Human Rights Watch reports tend to increase the risk of child marriage, can end a girl's education and effectively bar girls from entering the workforce and becoming fully autonomous.

In countries severely affected by AIDs and other sexually transmitted diseases, comprehensive, accurate sexual health education is just as life-saving. As early as one year after the gag rule was reinstated by the Trump administration, living standards in developing nations that relied on global support to address high maternal mortality rates and STI epidemics have already shown signs of worsening.

And on the domestic front, just over a year after reinstating the global gag rule, President Trump proposed a policy to permit doctors and health care providers in the U.S. to withhold information about abortion and birth control options from women on the grounds of religious freedom, even if doing so could endanger their patients' lives. Trump also announced his intent to strip organizations that offer abortion services—despite existing laws that prevent federal funding from paying for abortions—of Title X funding. Planned Parenthood clinics across the country offer family planning resources to 60 percent of all low-income people on Medicaid, according to 2014 data, making it clear who would be hit hardest.

Some may say that this is freedom—but whose freedom? It certainly isn't freedom for the women whose ill luck will see them served by doctors with misogynist biases or anti-choice religious beliefs, for women whose health care decisions and futures will be limited based on what they are or aren't told by a physician they place full trust in. After all, all women should be able to fully trust their doctors and health care providers.

A domestic gag rule would erode that trust, and for women without the privilege of being warned that their doctor isn't telling them the whole truth, the gag rule could erode their options and autonomy.

For anyone who opposes abortion or contraception, and refuses to discuss these resources and basic rights with vulnerable, disproportionately low-income women seeking care, freedom already exists—the freedom to choose a job that doesn't require them to tell women their full range of reproductive health options. Believe it or not, there are many jobs that don't require this. Part of being a health care provider is talking about health care—and regardless of what some ideological hardliners would have you believe, abortion *is* health care. Not murder, not politics, and certainly not something that any licensed doctor should legally be allowed to hide and lie about.

To tell women that censorship of the truth—and truth that could drastically alter the course of our lives, at that—is something as simple and innocent as freedom of speech is the epitome of gaslighting. It's dangerous and abusive; it presents an honest and damning portrait of modern patriarchy and its prioritization of the male perspective and experience of "freedom" over the livelihoods of women.

For certain, there are women doctors who oppose the right to have an abortion and want the right to not discuss this with patients. But that doesn't negate how this policy is being proposed by a male president and majority-male administration, and without any consideration of what freedom means for low-income women. The domestic gag rule is an act of male dominance, and is born of the notion that women's rights and autonomy are acceptable collateral damage for an inherently male construction of freedom.

TODAY, AS WE HAVE BEEN for centuries, women are screaming at the top of our lungs—on social media, in organized marches across the country, in everyday conversations, everywhere. But so much of the time nowadays, it feels like we aren't even screaming demands or asking for better anymore. Instead, so often it feels like we're simply screaming facts, established truths, objective realities that have increasingly come to be buried by lies, censorship, and anti-women ideologies.

We scream that restrictions on abortion will only increase unsafe abortions; we scream that only birth control and education will help reduce the need for abortions; we scream that abortion and miscarriage are different things; we scream that breast cancer, infertility, and depression are not consequences of abortion; we scream that your laws and violent ideologies are killing us.

We scream with the facts standing behind us—and patriarchal institutions standing perpetually against us.

HOW THE RIGHT USES
"PRO-LIFE" WOMEN TO GASLIGHT

In 2017, Media Matters for America released a study that showed 60 percent of all comments about abortion on cable news were made by men. Thus, it should be unsurprising that 64 percent of all cable news comments on abortion were also inaccurate.

And there seems to be a pattern here. Eighty percent of Congress is male and 75 percent of state legislatures comprise male lawmakers, as of 2017, and these numbers already mark the closest America has ever been to gender parity in politics. A study of all of the anti-abortion bills proposed in state legislatures in January 2017 revealed 71 percent had been introduced by white Republican men.

Persistent underrepresentation of women has steep, dangerous consequences for reproductive rights. But to be clear, everyone—not just women—suffers from the frustrating lack of female leadership opportunities in this country.

Political science research through the years has shown that women lawmakers, who on average introduce and pass almost double the number of bills their male counterparts do, tend to focus more on key domestic issues such as civil rights, education, and health care. Their inclusion in greater numbers is a vital antidote to the systemic culture of sexual harassment and exploitation by male superiors unveiled by the #MeToo movement, and their cognizance of what women and mothers experience in the workplace is absolutely requisite to passing meaningful legislation related to family leave and childcare.

In 2016, an all-male committee in Utah's state legislature rejected a bill to scrap the state tampon tax. In 2017, 13 male senators wrote the new Republican health bill, which would have allowed women who have given birth, been pregnant, or experienced rape and sexual abuse to be discriminated against by health care providers, had it passed.

We need more women who can understand the dire nature of being unable to afford menstrual hygiene products. After all, most men feel an almost deathly discomfort around tampons and are hardly in a position to understand how low-income women and girls' inability to access basic hygiene products is precisely the sort of barrier that often holds them back behind their male peers in academic and professional settings. Speaking broadly, we need more women in politics who can attest to how the health care system was made to exclude and discredit us.

Of course, I say all of this as someone who has been to my fair share of pro-choice rallies and protests, and stared in the faces of dozens of "pro-life" women with posters featuring bloodied fetuses, and "Women Deserve Better" signs. I'm not blind to the reality that Iowa Gov. Kim Reynolds signed the radical, anti-choice fetal heartbeat bill into law in 2018, or how the same study that showed 71 percent of anti-abortion laws were introduced by white Republican men also showed 25 percent of these laws were introduced by white Republican women.

Acknowledging the existence and substantial numbers of women who support policies that are counterproductive to their health, who gleefully accept what measly rights male leaders see fit to hand them, who bemoan feminists for exaggerating nonexistent problems, isn't fun. But I'm tired of these women being weaponized against feminism and abortion rights, and I'm tired of feminism, as author Jessica Valenti has so aptly put it, feminism is being co-opted by the right to mean "anything women say or do" rather than a defined set of principles for justice and human rights.

The fact that some women oppose abortion has no bearing on the indisputable reality that women die from unsafe abortions in the absence of safe, legal abortion. It does not change how the absence of safe, legal abortion means not only staggering numbers of maternal deaths, but also women being forced by the government to give birth, to give up their goals, dreams and economic security and effectively serve as state incubators. Feminism is not about advancing any one, singular woman, or one, singular class of women. Feminism is about what would benefit all women most, and that certainly isn't more lawmakers—regardless of their gender—voting against our rights and interests.

The amplification of conservative, anti-choice women's voices by the right is arguably the most dangerous form of gaslighting being deployed against us. As we have seen with the right's advocacy for Gina Haspel to be CIA director despite her jarring record on torture, and its demands for a "pro-life" woman to fill the Supreme Court vacancy left by Anthony Kennedy in July 2018, conservative politicians believe women can be reduced to shields in order to deflect sexism. And when feminists oppose the movement's "pro-life" female flag-bearers on the grounds of their beliefs and voting records, the right subsequently accuses us of being sexist.

Women on the right can be and often are victims of sexism. In multiple incidents, notably aired on Fox News, male commentators have made crude comments about Ivanka Trump's body with no relevance to her hypocritical stances and poisonous complicity. The right does not truly care about women's interests—not even the interests of its women supporters. It parades its female sympathizers with the goal of humiliating and aggravating feminists. A handful of reliable, token anti-choice women allows the movement to market blatantly harmful, misogynist policies as "women-approved."

This has especially been the case within the Trump administration, which has seen Press Secretary Sarah Huckabee Sanders stand behind a podium and explain to women—with ever so much feminist grace—why we would soon lose access to birth control in October 2017. Just one month later, she would very calmly explain to women that our sexual assaults should not be investigated or taken seriously until the male perpetrator himself confesses, unilaterally discrediting everyone who has ever experienced sexual abuse.

Ivanka, whose quiet dignity and femininity helped make her father digestible to 53 percent of white women voters in 2016, gave her stamp of approval to the Trump administration's slashing of an Obama-era directive that helped combat the gender wage gap in September 2017. In a book she penned some time before the #MeToo era, the first daughter claimed women who feel offended or harassed by commentary and behavior from men in the workplace should simply laugh it off; her father and brothers have suggested that if Ivanka were to experience harassment in the workplace, she would just go work somewhere else. Despite working in her father's administration as a senior adviser, she has routinely dismissed questions about the myriad allegations of assault against him by claiming such questions are unfair to ask of the president's daughter.

While profiting immensely from her father's campaign and victory, and gaining a platform to market herself as a supporter of women's empowerment, factories that produce Ivanka's clothing line exploit and abuse women, mothers, and children, according to a number of reports and lawsuits she has yet to publicly address. And according to the 2018 memoir of former Planned Parenthood President Cecile Richards, Ivanka, and her husband, Jared Kushner, once pressured and bribed Richards to decrease the number of abortions offered by Planned Parenthood to receive more—or rather, not lose—funding. Within months of the memoir's publication, President Trump announced his intent to strip Planned Parenthood of Title X funding. Not so much as a peep was heard from Ivanka.

Birth control and abortion are essential health care for women to succeed and experience economic enfranchisement as a unit in the workforce. The complicity of some women in taking birth control and reproductive health care away from other women does not somehow change the impact that this has on women as a whole. The visibility and airs of importance bestowed upon Sanders and Ivanka are not acts of feminism, but gaslighting by this administration, to tell women that if we feel hurt or attacked by the policies of an alleged sexual abuser, it's all in our heads: "Look at Sarah, look at Ivanka—women are doing just fine, and they're even smiling and happy, too; everything is fine for women, and real feminists don't self-identify as victims."

We've all heard adult men reference their wives and daughters and mothers and aunts and any and all women they've ever crossed paths with as testaments to just how not-sexist they are. And, of course, we've heard the underlying message to these long lists of women references: that men need familial female figures in their lives just to recognize that women are human beings. Similarly, the women of Trump's world are the vehicles through which this administration attempts to make its misogyny digestible, and pretend that it actually cares about women.

Kim Reynolds and the women leaders of anti-choice groups (like the very underhandedly named, "pro-life" Susan B. Anthony's List) are women—sure. But that does not reverse the patriarchal values inherent to the cause they are fighting for, a cause that says women who are pregnant and for any reason can't or do not want to be pregnant, have no choice. The anti-choice movement has one overarching goal, plain and simple, and that is forcing women to give birth. Whether it's men or women who comprise the movement's frontline of misogynist crusaders, it's a War on Women nonetheless.

In either case, it now seems worth reiterating that 25 percent of bills restricting abortion are introduced by white Republican women. Believe it or not, the experiences of wealthy, white, cisgender, heterosexual, able-bodied women are vastly different from those of women of color, low-income women, LGBTQ people, non-binary folks, differently abled women, and immigrant women. Women, across the board, share many experiences and face many of the same challenges—but certainly, some of us face identity-based challenges that others don't, especially when it comes to reproductive rights. In the days preceding *Roe v. Wade* and far too often, even today, it was and remains women of color, low-income women, immigrant women, and other marginalized people who are disproportionately blocked from accessing life-saving care.

It's black women who are 243 percent more likely than white women to die of pregnancy or birth-related causes. It's Central American migrant women, 60 to 80 percent of whom experience sexual assault while crossing the border, who are being held hostage in detainment centers and prohibited from accessing abortion by the Trump administration. It's Asian-American women who are stereotyped as likely to "kill" their "babies" on the basis of gender, and in several documented cases, have been jailed for the outcomes of their pregnancy in the U.S.

When it comes to many issues, but abortion, especially, white Republican women speak for white Republican women.

ONLY SLUTS NEED BIRTH CONTROL

I didn't know that birth control has only been legal for un-married women on the federal level in the U.S. since 1972 until relatively recently. I learned about the Supreme Court ruling of *Eisenstadt v. Baird* while working as an intern at NARAL Pro-Choice America, and at that point, I had been writing columns and articles about reproductive rights for more than three years. I don't have any good excuse for not knowing this, except that, like so many other women of reproductive age today, birth control is a part of my life. Today, in the U.S., more than 10.6 million women use birth control pills. The contraception mandate of the Affordable Care Act empowered 55 million women to gain access to copay-free, diverse forms of birth control.

In 2017, the Trump administration announced its intent to roll back the contraception mandate on the grounds that it violated the religious freedom of health insurers and employ-ers, and unilaterally offered them permission to deny women health care for any reason—even if said employers and insurers weren't religious, and just didn't like the idea of women having recreational sex. The policy decision, which yielded immedi-ate conflicts in institutions like Notre Dame University and businesses across the country, marked the ultimate perversion of religious freedom, allowing women to be denied safe, legal health care, solely for not sharing the values or religious views of their employers or insurers.

Birth control is a part of life for so many women, so much so that I'll admit I sometimes forget just how mired in misogynist, puritanical stigma it remains, today. Speaking as someone who's regularly written articles about birth control in women's magazines for the past few years, just as writing about abortion tends to draw your run-of-the-mill "baby killer" comments and emails, writing about birth control draws all kinds of slut-shaming, or, at the very least, civilly articulated arguments about why the taxpayer shouldn't have to pay for women's purported promiscuity.

Others cynically roll their eyes at the women who live in fear of losing access to birth control if Planned Parenthood is defunded or the Affordable Care Act is gutted, claiming birth control is already cheap and affordable for all. There's a reason Republicans in state legislatures have recently begun to join bipartisan efforts to make birth control available over-the-counter in some states, including even the persistently anti-choice Tennessee. And that reason has pretty much nothing to do with uplifting women, and everything to do with taking birth control away from poor women, who, without insurance, couldn't afford birth control whether over-the-counter or prescribed by a doctor.

To respond to these equal parts inaccurate and prevalent misconceptions, where do I even begin? Let's start by going back to 2017 when the nonprofit Child Trends released a study revealing the United States would save $12 billion in public health costs annually if every woman had access to the most reliable contraception. The Obama-era contraception mandate saved women in America $1.4 billion annually, and seeing as women comprise more than half of the U.S. population, it should go without saying how women saving money is good for the economy.

From a purely economic standpoint, public funding and coverage of birth control actually save the taxpayer money, in light of all the costs associated with assisting low-income children and families that our taxes would otherwise pay for. Around half of all births in the United States are paid for by Medicaid. The "economic argument" against free or at the very least subsidized birth control for all American women doesn't have a leg to stand on; it's just slut-shaming dressed as fiscal conservatism.

To my next point, birth control pills can cost $15 to $50 per month, which can be the difference between whether some women are able to eat enough and take care of themselves. And birth control pills aren't the only form of hormonal birth control. IUDs and implants, which are substantially more reliable, long-term and convenient, can cost up to $1,300 depending on your insurance provider. In other words, claims that women don't need free or subsidized birth control erase the experiences of low-income women, and render the ability to control one's body a privilege rather than a right.

And one serious problem with this is the fact that birth control is health care, and when health care becomes a privilege, women get sick and even die. The argument that birth control is inherently tied to sex and promiscuity—and, of course, that there is something inherently wrong with sex and promiscuity in so far as it is tied to women—is pure ignorance, deceit, and certainly, gaslighting.

Sure, your stereotypical nasty "sluts" need birth control, but guess what? So do women who struggle with health conditions so severe that pregnancy could endanger or end their lives. So do married women with children, struggling to provide for the children they already have, or simply not interested in expanding their families. The right's oversimplification of birth control and who needs birth control erase all of these women, and without even knowing us, tell the millions of American women seeking this basic health care that our motives are inherently corrupt and shameful.

In 2012, a Georgetown Law School graduate named Sandra Fluke testified before Democratic lawmakers (after being squarely denied by Republican representatives on the House Oversight and Government Reforms Committee) about the need for coverage of birth control in insurance plans. In her testimony drawing on her experiences and observations at Georgetown, she recalled a landscape in which "students pay as much as $1,000 a year out-of-pocket for a birth control prescription, a married woman stopped taking the pill because she couldn't afford it, and a friend needed the prescription for a medical condition unrelated to pregnancy but gave up battling to get it," according to *The Washington Post*. Fluke never once made any reference to her sex life.

But that didn't stop conservative commentator and evolution denier Rush Limbaugh from quite literally calling her a "slut" and "prostitute" in response to her testimony: "[Fluke] essentially says that she must be paid to have sex—what does that make her? It makes her a slut, right? It makes her a prostitute. She wants to be paid to have sex. She's having so much sex she can't afford the contraception. She wants you and me and the taxpayers to pay her to have sex," he said on his radio program.

Believe it or not, as ignorant, foul and plainly stupid as Limbaugh's comments were, they also blew a long-buried truth wide open. Slut-shaming was never *just* about stereotypes of sexually active teenage girls, or sex workers, or promiscuous women, in general. It's always been about all women, no matter their marital status or any other factors, who have sex, enjoy sex, and, radically enough, don't have sex solely to procreate. Limbaugh may have had college-age women in mind when he spoke about how women who want access to affordable birth control are "sluts" and "prostitutes," but his frame of logic includes married women, working mothers, women in long-term relationships, women with debilitating menstrual cycles, women who could die from conceiving a child.

His rant exposed how slut-shaming has never just been about sex, but degrading and invalidating all women who have it.

Of course, I hope my attempts to shine a light on the many women who need birth control for reasons other than the pursuit of non-committal sex don't come across as me, trying to distance birth control from the equally important women who are just trying to live their lives—lives rife with work, school, and, yes, sex. Women have sex. And while it's important to acknowledge the many women who use birth control to reduce severe menstrual cramps and heavy flow, or, you know, to survive, it's also important to acknowledge that birth control is also about sex, and that's just fine. More than fine. Birth control improves the living standards and conditions of women across the board and also empowers them to live confidently in their bodies, whatever that may look like for them.

In either case, Limbaugh may be a vocal misogynist, but he isn't the sole architect of a culture that demonizes sex and sexuality in women. Even well outside the landscape of reproductive rights policy, the stigmatization of female pleasure and the female experience of sex, in general, is rampant in media.

In 2018, Walmart pulled *Cosmopolitan* magazines from checkout lines, erroneously citing the #MeToo movement to justify its censorship of a women's magazine that focuses on representing women's authentic sexual experiences, and not only normalizing but also encouraging the experience of female pleasure.

Research through the years has shown that in film, depictions of women but not men receiving oral sex are more likely to be doomed to NC-17 ratings, which are effectively a death sentence for viewership. Films that portray literal beheadings are less likely to receive NC-17 ratings than films that portray women receiving head. This trend of erasure limits the reach and influence of films that portray female pleasure as a priority, and stigmatizes and discourages the inclusion of scenes that prioritize women's sexual experience in mainstream movies.

In 2016, Pornhub reported the second most viewed category among female audiences was gay porn. When asked, women respondents to a survey justified this preference by claiming gay porn dismantled the typical power dynamics exigent in heterosexual pornography, which largely sideline or erase the female experience altogether.

In other words, the male gaze is indisputably prioritized in today's media landscape, while female pleasure is either censored or at best, regarded as tangential. And, of course, sexual inequality transcends film: IRL, there exists a staggering gender orgasm gap. In 2009, when asked by the National Survey of Sexual Health and Behavior if they experienced orgasm during their last sexual encounter, 91 percent of men said yes, while just 64 percent of women said they did.

These failures of the media and reality together send a clear message: that sex was not made for women. The right's hostility toward birth control is a reflection of inherent, persistent sexual inequality, and a reflection of the dangerous, lived consequences of attaching shame and otherness to female sexuality in our culture.

When women have sex that is freely and consensually given, and also, for literally any reason, attempt to prevent pregnancy as a result of this, they are called "sluts" and "prostitutes," no additional context needed. And yet, those who shame female sexuality in safe, consensual contexts tend to be the same people who shame women for depriving men of sex, and blame women for the male rage and violence that is so often exacted upon society as a result of men being denied sex they feel entitled to.

The "incel," or "involuntary celibate," movement first rose to mainstream prominence and visibility in 2014, when 22-year-old Elliot Rodger killed seven in the Isla Vista shootings. A manifesto and series of videos by him revealed that his motive had been to punish women for not having sex with him, and punish the men whom women chose to sleep with, instead of him. His manifesto is additionally laden with racist language directing outrage at the men of color whom women choose to be with over white men.

According to most people who knew Rodgers, who identified as a virgin prior to his death, he had never made any real effort to connect or communicate with women, meaning they had never even really rejected him. Rather, he had just never put in any effort to develop relationships with women but had felt entitled to their bodies nonetheless. In the years prior to and following the Isla Vista shootings, nearly every perpetrator of a mass shooting has had a record of violence against women; at least two documented cases of mass shootings committed by men in the spring of 2018 had been related to feelings of rejection from women, with one act of mass violence in Toronto linked to a man who had shared incel content on his Facebook.

Rather than cede that there is a serious problem with gun laws in the United States, and all while scapegoating the mentally ill and offering no real solutions to their inadequate access to health care, the right often also blames gun violence on women. In the immediate aftermath of the Toronto attack, right-wing male thinkers took to the internet to suggest that the solution to all of this was according men the legal right to sex and women's bodies—some proposed this through government-funded sex robots for men (which is somehow less controversial than government-funded birth control), and even the "redistribution of sex" (no, the op-ed calling for this didn't run in *Breitbart*, but *The New York Times*.)

The sentiment that feeding and rewarding male notions of entitlement with women's bodies would somehow end mass, hypermasculine violence was shared by the Walk Up, Not Out movement, which identified the solution to mass school shootings like the Parkside shooting of 2018 as not gun control, but kindness. For starters, the two are hardly mutually exclusive. And while kindness is great, no woman has an obligation to "be kind" to any man she isn't interested in, or offer sexual favors and companionship to men who would otherwise go on to commit acts of mass violence in their communities. This would be an obvious recipe for domestic abuse and violence, and quite literally relegates women's bodies to human shields for the rest of society.

I spent most of my life thinking it was sex that conservatives took issue with. I grew up with two sisters, raised by two very old-fashioned, conservative parents, and so I never had brothers to watch them sexually police in the way they had, me and my sisters. It wasn't until I recognized how much sympathy the right has for violent, crazed male shooters rendered lonely by their inability to access women's bodies, and how little sympathy they have for literally any and all women seeking basic health care, that I finally understood.

If you believe men are entitled to women's bodies but women are not entitled to basic health care, you're part of the sexual inequality that reigns over every aspect of women's lives. If you choose to defend and advocate on behalf of men who commit violence in the name of being denied sex from women, all while ignoring how one in five women will experience sexual assault in her lifetime, then you stand on the frontlines of perpetuating that inequality.

No matter what anyone may tell you in defense of their stance against publicly funded birth control, we all must recognize that this perspective is inherently rooted in misogyny. We can't allow ourselves to be gaslit by patriarchal institutions and the men who stand with them about their true intentions, and their real, unfiltered perceptions of women and our health and sexuality. Opposition to our right to access birth control regardless of socioeconomic status is a direct manifestation of the War on Women, and its simultaneous disregard and disdain for the experience of female pleasure.

GASLIGHTING AND SEXUAL VIOLENCE

In the summer of 2018, two years after separating from actress Amber Heard, Johnny Depp settled a multimillion dollar lawsuit, which alleged that he had physically assaulted a location manager on the set of the film *City of Lies*. The news cycle stayed relatively mum throughout the ordeal, although, granted, there was far too much going on to give much focus to what was at that point run-of-the-mill behavior for Depp.

And yet, there was something deeply uncomfortable about the silence around this latest lawsuit accusing Depp of violent behavior. The lawsuit took place just two years after Depp's ex-wife Heard had accused him of domestic violence, armed with photographic evidence, witnesses, and no reason to lie. The actress, by all accounts, had tried to keep the divorce as quiet and as private as possible, but nonetheless, their separation and the story of a relationship rocked by repeated, persistent violence erupted into a national he-said-she-said. And even as Heard, who was wealthy in her own right, donated all money she received from the settlement to charity, and actively tried to maintain a low-profile, accusations that she had lied for attention, for money, or to exact some sort of revenge on Depp persisted.

We heard none of these same accusations directed at Gregg Brooks, the location manager allegedly assaulted by Depp, who likely opted to keep all or most of the money he received from the settlement. And this double standard is really just the tip of the iceberg in terms of continued inequality in our conversations around sexual assault, despite claims of how dangerous society supposedly now is for "falsely accused" men. Men are more likely to experience sexual assault themselves than to be falsely accused of committing it.

Researchers say that false reports comprise just 2 to 8 percent of all reports of sexual assault, although it's anyone's guess what, exactly, constitutes "false reporting." After all, far too many "false reports" involve both parties agreeing that a sexual encounter happened, and simply disputing whether or not one party felt violated.

Today, a jarring false equivalence is being made between the power dynamics of survivors who come forward and men who are accused, threatening to stifle all progress survivors' rights groups have made in recent years as men attempt to weaponize and appropriate victimhood. Men's fears of being "falsely accused"—as if that's something that *really*, actually happens—and women's fears of being raped and killed, are vastly different, and vastly unequal. The notion that women and survivors are now in a predatory position is a construct of male revisionism, of gaslighting by patriarchal institutions to halt feminist attempts at making society safer and more equitable for women.

Gaslighting has always been a staple of sexual violence and domestic abuse; victims who are in long-term relationships with their abusers are often manipulated into believing that what they are experiencing is normal, not that bad, or somehow their fault, or that the repeated episodes of abuse are isolated and not part of a broader trend. And gaslighting in dialogues around sexual violence takes form in the notion that men have somehow become the victims, just because they now feel insecure and self-conscious about practicing predatory behaviors that have literally always been wrong. Despite the critically important nature and progress of #MeToo, a movement that has elevated and exposed the prevalence of women's experiences with sexual exploitation and abuse, survivors continue to face marginalization in our culture and legal system.

The revelations of #MeToo have held up a mirror to systemic sexual violence committed and enabled by famous and powerful men since, well, forever, across all industries in which famous and powerful men remain the gatekeepers to success. And for all the critically important accusations that have come to light ever since the first major report about the behavior of Harvey Weinstein, convictions and real consequences beyond social ostracism have been limited. Wealthy men remain for the most part untouchable, and above any meaningful consequences and accountability for the trauma and degradation to which they subject their female victims.

#MeToo is powerful because women and survivors are powerful. The movement we've built together is a force to be reckoned with. But the power of #MeToo is not predatory, it is driven by justice, solidarity, and a righteous demand for men to be held accountable for their words, actions, and treatment of women. And simultaneously, #MeToo's power remains vastly challenged by patriarchal institutions, attitudes, and narratives, despite how terrifying and eclipsing the movement's male opponents claim that it is.

Anyone who says that #MeToo has gone too far isn't paying

attention—not to the women it's helped uplift, not to the workplaces it's changed to be safer and more inclusive, and certainly not to women's experiences, in general. #MeToo is only frightening to the men who know they have caused women in their lives to feel violated at some point, and today, are unwilling to listen to our voices about how we want to be treated going forward. And yet, it's precisely these men and their sympathizers who hold the reins of our cultural conversations around systemic sexual abuse, and with these reins in their hands, are attempting to gaslight, deceive, discredit and silence us.

Our understanding of women's experiences and interactions with men have always been governed by men and their rewriting and gaslighting. And today, we see that in cultural perceptions of #MeToo as dangerous.

Anti-#MeToo fearmongerers ignore how the realities and gendered double standards faced by Amber Heard remain the norm for most women, despite the undeniable progress #MeToo has facilitated. They portray women's gains and the general pro-equality direction society is moving toward as an existential threat to men, simply because we are working to reshape a culture that has for too long given men broad permission to treat women however they want. They tell us the pendulum has swung too far so that men are now being persecuted, and in doing so, they erase the reality of an epidemic of violence against women that is vastly enabled by politicians and cultural leaders, and erase how survivors' options for fair recourse remain vastly limited.

Despite the narrative that women only accuse famous men for attention and money, survivors have everything to lose and nothing to gain from coming forward—that is, nothing that could be of greater value than their safety, the safety of their loved ones, and their reputations. In 2017, an Alabama woman who had accused former U.S. Senate candidate and far-right icon Roy Moore of sexually assaulting her as a teenager, saw her house burned down in an act identified by law enforcement as arson.

In 2016, a slew of accusations of sexual harassment and assault were lodged against then-candidate Donald Trump in the weeks after *The Washington Post* published audio of Trump in 2004 boasting about "[grabbing]" women "by the pussy," and initiating sexual encounters with married women, with or without their consent.

As of 2018, more than 20 employees, work associates, contestants on his 2000's reality show, beauty pageant contestants, reporters and other women have accused Trump of groping them, harassing them, assaulting them, and cornering and threatening them into silence. Many of these women even had witnesses, who corroborated. Trump, himself, boasted about committing the very same behaviors his accusers described in the 2004 tape.

Prior to the slew of allegations in 2016, in the summer of 2015, since-redacted accusations of rape and domestic abuse against Trump by his first wife Ivana came to light, sparking crude debate about whether husbands could legally rape their wives; Trump's lawyer Michael Cohen resoundingly argued that no, they couldn't. Apparently, for women, marriage means the forfeiture of their humanity, as they become pieces of property in the eyes of Trump and the men who work for him.

Perhaps the most fundamental aspect of consent, beyond how it must be freely given, is that it's a one-time thing, on an encounter-by-encounter basis. Trump's alleged inability to recognize this as Ivana's husband, as well as his personal lawyer's very public refusal to recognize this, should have robbed Trump of any credibility in his claims about sexual assault going forward.

But the accusations issued against him in October 2016 spanned over the course of decades and were lodged while Trump was not only squarely in the limelight, but also a month away from the general election. While many questioned or outright disbelieved the accusations against Trump in light of these circumstances, brushing them off as stunts to influence the election, others recognized that the women had come forward because this was the only moment they could really be credible—after Trump, their male alleged abuser, had broadly confessed to assault in a tape we all heard. Comedian Bill Cosby had also been accused of assault by dozens of women over the course of his career, and even confessed to using date rape drugs in court, only to remain a free man for years before women were finally believed. Trump's very own press secretary once stated in October 2017 that reports of sexual assault should only be investigated if the male perpetrator first confesses, essentially robbing all women and survivors of credibility.

The dialogue around accusations against Trump should have been about whether we believed Trump, himself, and took him at his word when he boasted about grabbing women's genitalia without their consent. Instead, he and his supporters and campaign staff went into overdrive attacking the characters of the many private women who had risked everything to inform the electorate about the true character of a man who might become our president. He attacked their appearances and personal lives at rallies before crowds numbering in the thousands, making it clear as day why an estimated 62 to 84 percent of assaults go unreported, and subsequently, why, as #MeToo has revealed in Hollywood and American politics alike, famous men continue to get away with abusing female subordinates.

Male dominance across every industry and an overarching culture of complicity to maintain this dominance has long silenced unsaid numbers of women. And when they have wealth and power, accused men are able to utilize their vast platforms and influence to publicly destroy or excommunicate any woman who speaks against them, establishing an impenetrable culture of silence among women and victims who are often just trying to survive in their fields or keep themselves and their loved ones out of the public eye. Just to conceal a *consensual* affair, Trump allegedly threatened to hurt actress Stormy Daniels and her child if she told their story, Daniels has said. And this silence imposed on women by their attackers ultimately helps protect male perpetrators from facing accountability, resulting in the vast majority of perpetrators becoming repeat offenders.

But it's not just victims of famous, wealthy men who face terrifying and degrading challenges upon coming forward. According to a study by the United States Bureau of Justice Statistics published in 2007, general fear of disbelief and punishment, of being forced to relive their trauma to prove their experiences in an extended bureaucratic process, and, more than anything, being disbelieved, shamed, ostracized, or potentially harassed by law enforcement, lead many survivors to "choose" silence.

No matter the status of the perpetrator, in nearly all cases of sexual assault, the only evidence a survivor can really provide is their own testimony. Believe it or not, most people aren't wearing body cameras everywhere they go to capture "proof" of their every experience. Many sexual assaults take place without witnesses or DNA evidence, or are reported after too much time has passed for survivors to provide evidence beyond their testimony.

The fact that credibility is inherently, polarizingly gendered means reporting has never really been an option for most survivors. And certainly, none of this should be interpreted to exclude male, trans or nonbinary survivors, who are just as often discredited on the basis of gender, and subjected to crass jokes meant to erase and belittle their experiences.

If sexual assaults are reported at all, understandably, they are often reported after substantial time has elapsed since the encounter. And the longer survivors delay the reporting process, the more tangible evidence they're likely to lose, and the less credibility they have with authorities presiding over their cases. That's one key reason survivors' rights advocates have been calling for the repeal of statutes of limitation for crimes of sexual abuse in states across the country.

One of the most prominent examples of how the criminal justice system's evidentiary standards inherently work against survivors exists in the notorious case of Brock Turner. On January 18, 2015, while a student athlete at Stanford University, Turner sexually assaulted an unconscious woman until witnesses caught him and called the police. In the immediate aftermath of the assault, the young woman, called Emily Doe, was taken to the hospital and Turner's DNA was collected from her body as evidence against him.

Over the course of Doe's trial, there was never any question of whether Turner had assaulted her. She had been unconscious and could not testify to her own experiences, but witnesses and Turner's DNA certainly could. And yet, the trial dragged on, awash with victim-blaming questioning about Doe's attire, diet, sexual history, and drinking history, leading up to then-County Judge Aaron Persky's decision to sentence Turner to just six months in county jail. Turner would wind up serving just three of those months, before being released early for "good behavior" and picking up where his life left off.

Persky's rationale had been that prison time and prolonged incarceration would have "severe impact" on Turner, as if Turner's assault of an unconscious woman did not have "severe impact" on her. Within two years of his decision, Santa Clara County voters would vote to recall Persky from his post in direct response to his repeated failure to hold sexual abusers accountable and maintain safety and respect for survivors in his court.

To the point, even when survivors seemingly have everything it should take to be believed and accorded justice, many will still face the same indignities Doe was subjected to, nonetheless.

One in five women will be raped at some point in their lives, according to the National Sexual Violence Resource Center; Native American women and girls are 2.5 times more likely than all other women to experience sexual assault. Sexual violence is endemic in society, and in response to this, we consistently fail to accord survivors the resources or show them the compassion they need to seek and receive justice, or experience healing.

And while the concept of false accusations is certainly concerning, nonetheless, I've been alarmed by the extent to which ignorance surrounds this issue.

In 2017, I had the pleasure of speaking with the author of

Blurred Lines: Rethinking Sex, Power, and Consent on Campus. In an enlightening conversation about her book and its myriad landmark findings, Vanessa Grigoriadis told me what most people continue to miss when it comes to campus sexual assault: On college campuses, for every accusation of assault, there is nearly always consensus that a sexual encounter took place, with one party saying that they felt violated by the encounter. There are seldom cases in which one party disputes that there was an encounter. In other words, the epidemic of sexual violence is certainly perpetuated by male dominance and lack of accountability at large, but it may also be a product of dangerous, widespread ignorance about consent, which has subsequently inflicted disproportionate trauma on women and girls, and is inextricably bound to the gendered nature of credibility.

Ignorance about consent arguably stems from male entitlement and privilege within heterosexual relationships and encounters. For women in these circumstances, the nuances of consent are often the difference between safety and violence. Lack of consent education in most sex education programs—when schools offer sexual education, at all—suggests men are just entitled to sex and women's bodies without having to ask. The failure to teach men how to ask for sex reflects a system that enables male entitlement to sex on demand, no permission necessary.

In either case, let's consider, once again, the overarching media narrative that cultural shifts to acknowledge the prevalence of sexual violence are somehow dangerous for men. Consider some of the most iconic headlines about #MeToo, published between 2017 and 2018: "When the #MeToo movement goes too far," "Weinstein and #MeToo: 'confused' men could shy away from hiring women," "Young single Americans are tired, confused and scared about dating during #MeToo," "Henry Cavill Worries #MeToo Is Preventing Men From Wooing Women Out of Fear of Being Called a 'Rapist'."

Perhaps men are confused. Perhaps men are afraid. But it's no accident that their fears, their confusion, and their perspective, in general, remain the priority, even in media coverage of a fundamentally women-centered movement. Feminist writer Rebecca Solnit put it best in her April 2018 essay, "Whose Story (and Country) is this?", when she wrote:

> "We've heard from hundreds, perhaps thousands, of women about assaults, threats, harassment, humiliation, coercion, of campaigns that ended careers, pushed them to the brink of suicide. Many men's response to this is sympathy for men. … But the follow-up story to the #MeToo upheaval has too often been: how do the consequences of men hideously mistreating women affect men's comfort? Are men okay with what's happening? There have been too many stories about men feeling less comfortable, too few about how women might be feeling more secure in offices where harassing coworkers may have been removed or are at least a bit less sure about their right to grope and harass. Men themselves insist on their comfort as a right …"

The male experience has long been the default, and a movement conceived to shine a light on women's experiences should not be usurped by male cynicism. What we are seeing is a deeply condescending false equivalence, one that suggests that a proven culture of misogynist violence and abuse long erased from the public eye is somehow the same evil as—God forbid—accountability for abusive men, or the same evil as men now being forced to—God forbid—consider how their actions could cause women to feel.

The preservation of a man's reputation and feelings of safety are always given priority when women accuse men of assault. We saw this in the 2016 case of Brock Turner in Judge Aaron Persky's concern with the "severe impact" that years in prison could have on Turner, but not the "severe impact" his actions had had on his female victim.

In treating accused men as if they're the ones being victimized and oppressed, we create a false equivalence between holding male abusers accountable and the traumatic experience of sexual assault. We suggest that two entirely different experiences are somehow comparable, that the act of assaulting someone and the act of coming forward are somehow equally oppressive behaviors. And just as dangerously, we suggest that sexual assault is something women would lie about merely to victimize men. The appropriation of victimhood by men accused of sexual assault isn't just cruel and misguided; it places survivors in abject danger.

THE SYSTEMIC GASLIGHTING of women and survivors extends beyond the cultural and is codified into laws and policies on nearly every level of government. As of 2017, the male victimization narrative is effectively the official policy of the Trump Education Department, which has spent every day since January 20, 2017, launching a full 180 from the progress of the Obama era.

Under President Obama, the Education Department

required schools receiving federal funding to follow a set of critically important policies to protect the rights of sexual assault survivors. Namely, these policies included a lower evidentiary standard for survivors to prove their experiences, taking into consideration how many survivors simply lack the capacity to provide evidence beyond their testimony. Additionally, the Obama Education Department called for schools to close investigations of assault in a timely manner, stating the typical investigation length should be within 60 days.

As of 2017, Trump's education secretary Betsy DeVos has moved to collapse both policies, equating the very real prevalence of campus sexual assault with men's rights groups' claims of mass false reporting. DeVos first announced these policy changes in a disturbing September 2017 speech, in which she touted a few specific, highly complicated cases meant to promote fearmongering about false reporting. DeVos additionally stated she would revoke the 60-day guideline, disregarding the crucial pressure it placed on universities to actually handle reports with a sense of urgency, and instead claimed that rigid deadlines could cause sloppiness. She has yet to acknowledge how the majority of assaults still often go unreported, nor offer any insight into how a higher evidentiary standard somehow, magically, wouldn't discourage survivors from reporting.

Campus sexual assault is treated as a Title IX issue due to its disparate potential to derail women's academic careers, and inflict trauma, mental illness, and general terror on young women in universities, not to mention, cause unsaid numbers of young women to struggle with their academics or drop out of school altogether. When fewer survivors report due to lack of protection of their rights, fewer predators—who tend to be repeat offenders—will be expelled from universities, making campuses become dangerous landscapes as a result of these negligent, deeply harmful policies. The Trump Education Department's prioritization of the male experience over women and survivors' safety, well-being and livelihood shows just how dangerous gaslighting can be when it shapes the policies that govern our lives.

The Trump administration's meninist hijacking of the Education Department is just one example of its proactive protection of male abusers, and subsequently, its war on survivors. As of the first two years of Trump's presidency, Trump has neglected to name a leader to head the Justice Department's Office on Violence Against Women. And speaking of the Justice Department, Attorney General Jeff Sessions personally saw to the administration's 2018 policy of denying asylum to victims of domestic violence from Central America, which is effectively a death sentence for unsaid numbers of women and mothers, and a reflection of the disparate experiences of women of color with sexual violence.

In 2018, *The New York Times* reported that the Trump administration's rhetoric and aggressively racist immigration policies have discouraged undocumented women subjected to sexual violence from reporting, out of fear of deportation and punishment. The increased militarization of the Southern border has also helped to yield a high risk of sexual violence for migrant women and girls, 60 to 80 percent of whom experience sexual assault in the process of crossing the border.

Despite this, the Justice Department has repeatedly argued cases to allow the Trump administration to deny abortion care to pregnant women and girls in detainment centers, even in cases of rape. The justification for this outlandishly cruel policy has thus far been that non-citizen women and girls are not entitled to the human rights of citizens, and granting them basic health care would "incentivize" more border-crossers— as oppose to, say, the violence in their home countries that forces many Central American women to cross the border in the first place.

All while sweepingly identifying Mexican immigrants as "rapists," Trump has quite literally gone out of his way to hire alleged domestic abusers and vocally, publicly defend them. The epically long list of accused men Trump at some point hired between his campaign and presidential administration includes, most recently, former White House secretary Rob Porter, former speechwriter David Sorensen, former chief strategist Steve Bannon, former Labor Secretary nominee Andrew Puzder, and former campaign manager Corey Lewandowski. In the fall of 2018, it was revealed Trump's Supreme Court nominee Brett Kavanaugh had allegedly sexually assaulted or abused several women while he was in high school and college.

After the optics around Porter and Sorensen's records resulted in Chief of Staff John Kelly—who allegedly knew at least of the allegations against Porter before Porter was hired—firing both men in February 2018, President Trump wrote on Twitter: "Peoples [sic] lives are being shattered and destroyed by a mere allegation. Some are true and some are false. Some are old and some are new. There is no recovery for someone falsely accused - life and career are gone. Is there no such thing any longer as Due Process?"

Of course, bemoaning the death of "due process" and "innocence until proven guilty," all while offering no suggestions for what evidence survivors could provide that would sufficiently count as "proof" of their perpetrator's guilt, is truly something else coming from Trump. As a presidential candidate and now as president, Trump consistently leads chants of "lock her up!" at his political rallies about a female political opponent who has not been indicted for anything. (On the other hand, numerous higher-ups on Trump's presidential campaign and in his staff have been indicted for crimes or are in prison.) This hypocrisy should make it clear that Trump and his base's refusal to believe survivors has never been about a noble yearning to uphold and protect the Constitution, and has always been about degrading women, spitting in our faces, and empowering men to do whatever they want without consequences.

In either case, Trump's tweet brought attention back to Trump himself, whether or not this was his intent, and his own track record of dozens of allegations of abuse against him. It also raised a critical question: If not by their own testimony, then how, exactly, are survivors of assault supposed to prove their experiences? In addition to stereotyping Mexican immigrants as rapists in his campaign announcement speech, Trump's record of commenting on sexual assault also includes buying a full-page ad to accuse a group of black men—the Central Park Five—of a rape they had been exonerated from through DNA evidence, back in the 1990s. So, to answer my own question, perhaps one way survivors can prove their experiences to Trump is by accusing men of color.

Another way, as described by Press Secretary Sarah Huckabee Sanders in November 2017, could be through procuring a direct, explicit and public confession from your male abuser. Sanders once claimed that what differentiated accusations of sexual abuse against Trump from those against then-Minnesota Sen. Al Franken, a Democrat, were that Franken had confessed to some of the allegations. She proceeded to double-down on this argument, and state that we should only investigate cases in which the alleged perpetrator has publicly owned up to their actions. Conveniently enough, she made no mention of the 2004 audio of Trump, himself, callously bragging about acts that classify as sexual assault.

The president's unapologetic support and sympathy for alleged male abusers who are consistently welcomed into his administration, and whom he has consistently used the platform and influence of his office to defend, are by no means an anomaly within the Republican Party. Trump's decision to campaign for and defend former Alabama U.S. Senate candidate Roy Moore against multiple credible allegations of assaulting then-teenage girls in his hometown decades ago, was reinforced by the Republican National Committee's continued fundraising efforts for Moore. Additionally, Republican Senate Majority Leader Mitch McConnell refused to ask Moore to drop out of the race.

In addition to the Party's decision to stand with Roy Moore, conservative commentators filed onto cable news panels to argue that abortion—not assaulting born, living girls—was the real "child abuse." And none of this should have been surprising. The Republican Party has a long, colorful legislative history of either failing or blatantly attacking survivors and women. In 2013, 22 Republican senators voted against the renewal of the Violence Against Women Act in protest of its added protections for LGBTQ people and immigrants, and, as *The Atlantic* reported at the time, what Republicans perceived as a "feminist" attack on "family values."

Notably, access to the resources provided by the Violence

Against Women Act can be life or death for women and survivors. The law requires law enforcement to respond to reports of domestic violence in a timely manner, funds community violence prevention programs and resources for survivors (such as a national hotline, legal aid, and rape kit funding), establishes life-saving protections for victims who lose their homes due to incidents related to domestic violence, and offers services specifically for women with disabilities.

On the state level, one particularly jarring episode of Republican lawmakers attacking the rights and resources of survivors took place at a Georgia town hall in the summer of 2017. Rep. "Buddy" Carter told constituents he would only support funding for rape kit collection and processing in cities that complied with immigration laws, and would see that sanctuary cities were denied crucial funding to take care of survivors. As of 2018, tens of thousands of rape kits across the country are collected and left untested, backlogged for years or forever; in the few states like Colorado and Wisconsin that have invested extensively in testing rape kits and working to end backlogging, we have seen this yield dozens of new leads and convictions in rape cases.

The Republican Party's attacks on rape kit legislation haven't been limited to the equal-parts misogynist and xenophobic threats of Rep. Carter, who also famously threatened to "snatch a knot in their ass," referring to two female senators who said they would vote against repealing the Affordable Care Act in 2017. In 2015, Senate Republicans stalled a $180 billion funding bill that would invest $41 million in helping states and local governments process rape kits, jeopardizing the bill due to its protections of the environment. And it's not just rape kits: Republican senators also would have seen rape and sexual assault survivors denied health care or discriminated against by insurance providers through their 2017 health bill, which would have allowed surviving sexual assault and other traumas to be regarded as pre-existing conditions.

The Republican Party's War on Women famously refers to its attacks on reproductive health care, and it's important to recognize how these attacks often specifically target rape survivors. While some 16 percent of Americans have said they oppose abortion in all circumstances, including when pregnancy is caused by rape, a majority of anti-choice Republican senators often support exceptions to bans and restrictions on abortion that allow women impregnated by rape to elect to have abortions. But these "exceptions" exist solely to help anti-abortion laws appear less cruel and dangerous than they really are. In reality, abortion rape exceptions require survivors to prove their traumatic experiences and communicate with law enforcement or doctors whether they want to or not, just to receive health care that should be a right.

And what more could we really expect from the Party of Todd Akin, the former Missouri Congressman and U.S. Senate candidate who coined the term "legitimate rape" in 2012? Legitimate rape, of course, refers to the Akin's idea that women who are subjected to "real" rape will naturally be unable to conceive. Akin may be one politician, and certainly, plenty of Democratic men have been outed as abusers (though these men are often quickly condemned and disavowed by the rest of the Democratic Party, I might add.) And yet, in either case, Akin's disregard for the real, lived experiences of rape survivors is pretty much codified within the Republican Party platform.

Misogyny and abject cruelty are not glitches within the

Republican Party or Trump administration; they are deliberate and foundational to what both stand for. Men like Trump owe their electoral victories to rabid sexism, and specifically, to policy platforms promising the subjugation, oppression and humiliation of American women as a unit. Restrictions on our reproductive rights are acts of implicit but powerful sexual violence. These laws empower the physical control of women's bodies by the government without our consent, and physically hurt and endanger us by increasing our risk of facing pregnancy-related, life-threatening health complications.

In the same vein, the perpetuation of violence against women is—intentionally or not—a consequence of a number of key legislative stances held by Republican politicians.

For example, an American woman is shot by her partner every 16 hours, and victims of domestic violence are five times more likely to be killed if their abuser has access to a firearm. Fifty-seven percent of mass shootings, or shootings that result in at least four people killed with a gun, are initiated by a male abuser seeking to hurt his domestic partner. In other words, every year, thousands of women are killed quite literally for telling men "no."

Nearly every major mass shooting in this country has been executed by men with records and criminal histories of violence against women. And as we learn more about the incel movement and its encouragement of violence against women, it's become increasingly clear that male entitlement to women's bodies, paired with vastly accessible firearms, is a safety hazard—for society, for bystanders, for police officers involved, and above all, for women. When National Rifle Association-backed GOP lawmakers refuse to act and support common-sense gun control, their inaction enables mass violence of a distinctly gendered nature.

In 2017, the inauguration of President Trump spelled Republican Party dominance across all three branches of government. One of two major political parties in the U.S., and the one in power, no less, consistently capitalizes on its majority power to exact or enable violence against women: through reproductive coercion, inaction on gun control, and failure to support survivors. Violence against women and the empowerment of systemic, gendered abuse is codified into our culture, our legal system, our politics, our government.

And yet, the masking of this reality behind a theater of male insecurity and mass, often male privilege-fueled outrage serves to gaslight all of us about the ongoing realities of sexual violence.

IN THE SUMMER OF 2018, President Trump appointed a former Fox News executive ousted from the company for aiding and abetting sexual abuse by men like Roger Ailes and Bill O'Reilly for years. In response, *New York Times* columnist Michelle Goldberg put it best when she wrote, "Without the force of law behind it, #MeToo can create change only in institutions that are susceptible to shame, and the Trump administration is shameless. After all, if Trump cared about the American people's consent, he'd resign."

What cultural power and social ostracism can truly achieve is limited in the absence of meaningful legal policies to protect women. And the current lack of such policies is the direct result of male sexual predators and their enablers saturating spaces of political decision-making power.

Anyone who thinks #MeToo has gone "too far" isn't paying

attention—specifically, to women's voices. We need to hear women's voices amplified in media over patriarchal gaslighting and revisionism; we need women leaders to comprise the roles and spaces that male predators use to abuse, exploit and hide; and we need a mobilized electorate of women and allies that recognizes #MeToo is more than a cultural movement—it's the political fight of our lives, on every level of government.

AT THE END OF THE DAY, I'm nothing if not aware that codifying additional, necessary protections for sexual assault survivors and accountability measures for perpetrators into the law is a difficult sell in patriarchal society. The rallying cry of "innocent until proven guilty" is pretty difficult to argue with, because, of course, I and other supporters of survivors' rights support due process. Portraying survivors' rights advocates as opponents of the institution of due process is and always has been a rhetorical home run for sympathizers of rapists and accused men.

It should go without saying how this framing of our advocacy reflects a gross oversimplification of the nuance of consent. Nearly anyone with even an ounce of sexual experience, or sexually active friends who confide in them, could attest to how naturally gray areas tend to arise in sexual encounters. What sexual assaults so often boil down to is the often ineffable feeling and visceral, devastating sense of being violated—sometimes even if the other party doesn't feel they've done anything wrong. And such situations often arise as a result of inadequate or nonexistent consent education, a systemic issue that has disproportionately endangered women, girls and LGBTQ people for generations. Consent isn't complicated: It's freely given without coercion, can be withdrawn at any time, and must be affirmative and explicit. And if it isn't all these things, it isn't consent.

In either case, how do you provide physical, tangible evidence of the feeling of being violated? As a woman, how do you vocalize your discomfort or reject sexual advances in a manner that is clear and explicit, and simultaneously satisfies the internal requirements we have been socialized to place on ourselves, to be gentle and prioritize men's comfort above our own?

I often think about the story of one anonymous woman's described date night experience with Aziz Ansari, first made public in January 2018. There was outcry and backlash on all sides, and I say "all sides" because there were certainly more than two. It was complicated. But one thing was clear: Ansari had repeatedly refused to accept verbal and non-verbal cues that his date did not want sex, or interpreted her rejections as "convince me's." In nearly all things and especially in sexual encounters, "no" should never mean "convince me"—adult men like Ansari have a responsibility to know this.

While many were quick to point out and criticize Ansari's failure to respect his date's comfort, others condescendingly stated the obvious—that his actions did not constitute rape, as if women actually need men to explain what is or isn't rape to us. And in either case, the legality or illegality of an act doesn't necessarily dictate whether it is moral.

I and many women have shared the experiences of Ansari's date before. When I was a bit younger than I am now, less versed in affirmative consent, and more mentally and emotionally vulnerable, I'd internalized that sexual encounters that involved emotional pressure and discomfort were normal.

Of course, sexual assaults can sometimes be simple: There is a very explicit lack of consent, or someone is unconscious, something awful like that. But in plenty of other cases, women may find themselves feeling confused about what they just experienced, unsure if they were violated, unsure of how they feel, unsure of what they want to do next.

Survey after survey of sexually active men shows that a terrifying amount of men regularly practice behaviors that constitute sexual assault without even realizing or acknowledging this reality. The fact that men continue to practice these same behaviors without facing consequences or confrontation is a clear indicator of the disparity between sexual assaults, and reporting and accountability for assaults.

The survey's findings also reflect a frustrating, age-old trend. Often, the people who respond to women's commentary about rape culture with the slogan, "Not all men!", are the same people who shrug off behaviors constituting sexual assault with the mantra, "boys will be boys." How callously rape sympathizers are able to switch gears from "Not all men" to quite literally "Yes, all men." And clearly, there are lasting repercussions to this: When sexual assault is laughed off as boys being boys, young men are never able to learn that what they're doing is wrong, and continue to practice these terrifyingly normalized behaviors.

The pervasive, internalized idea among women that our experience in sex is of a lesser priority than men's, even in consensual scenarios, has led many women who feel violated by sexual encounters to immediately question this feeling or succumb to self-doubt. We question if we're being too sensitive, if it's all in our heads, if it's our fault for not being more assertive, rather than the fault of our partner for failing to be receptive and respectful of our hesitation.

Ultimately, my question for the "innocent until proven guilty" faction of sympathizers for sexual abusers is always the same: What do you regard as acceptable evidence for survivors to adequately prove their veracity? Documented, high-resolution footage of the assault taking place, the victim audibly and repeatedly screaming "no" throughout the assault, the perpetrator's face in clear view? Rape kits, the majority of which are backlogged by the thousands and never tested, or are not applicable to assaults that did not involve penetrative rape? What will it take for you to believe women? Every woman on Earth coming forward and saying that they, too, were assaulted by this same man?

These questions are only partially rhetorical. At this point, I really, sincerely want to know.

IT DIDN'T END WITH MARRIAGE EQUALITY

Women and the LGBTQ community have always stood in solidarity in a shared fight for bodily autonomy and the end of oppressive, heteronormative gender roles assigned by the patriarchy. It was never just women who were attacked and stripped of rights by patriarchal norms, but everyone across the spectrum of gender and orientation who deigned to break with traditional concepts of expression and identity.

Conservative revulsion with same-sex marriage, or what is now more widely and appropriately referred to as marriage equality, has always stemmed from naked homophobia, and an attachment to obligatory heterosexuality and an age-old desire to punish those who are different. But, as per the term "marriage equality," the right also rejects gay marriage because it signals the erosion of traditional, obligatory gender roles within the institution of marriage itself, subverting the ideas that dominance and heading a household are traditionally male roles, and what we give and take within marriage and romantic relationships is inherently gendered.

Marriage equality became the law of the land in the summer of 2015, where it had previously existed only in select states prior to the Supreme Court ruling of *Obergefell v. Hodges*. The decision was a triumph for inclusivity and human rights, especially as it took place at a time of increasing media and political representation of LGBTQ people. But for far too many people, it also seemed to mark a false end-game for LGBTQ rights.

The right bemoaned how everyone had all of a sudden become gay, how being gay had suddenly become "cool," just because the country had progressed to a point in which, in many places, LGBTQ people no longer encountered the same pressures to hide, censor and erase themselves. In many communities and households, of course, this remains a far-cry from reality. Despite undeniable progress, which is the product of generations of LGBTQ people and allies speaking out, fighting, and dying for their rights over the course of generations, what the LGBTQ community continues to face in this country is still frankly terrifying and unjust. And in lock-step with its policies and rhetoric affecting all marginalized groups, the Trump administration has really only made things worse.

PRIDE HAS ALWAYS WELCOMED and included allies. But far too many liberal-leaning straight people show up exclusively for that one weekend of the year. Perhaps we can't expect everyone to fit volunteering at LGBTQ youth shelters into their schedules, or fitting monthly donations to the Human Rights Campaign in tight budgets. But it shouldn't be too much to ask straight allies to educate themselves about the struggles and oppression this community continues to face.

In 2018, the Ad Council launched the campaign "Beyond I Do" to spotlight the continued oppression of LGBTQ people in the years after *Obergefell*. Thirty-one states as of 2018 continue to allow legal discrimination against members of the LGBTQ community on the grounds of religious freedom, meaning gay couples could get married one day and legally be fired by homophobic bosses, the next. They could legally be evicted from their apartments, denied service, or, more likely for trans people, be thrown out of restrooms.

The right's hijacking of "religious freedom" to promote an agenda of bigotry and intolerance is nothing new; it's plagued reproductive rights for years, justifying discriminatory barriers on poor women's access to crucial, legal health care like birth control and abortion.

From the perspective of right-wing politicians, "religious freedom" speaks exclusively to the experiences of people who adhere to traditional societal norms—or, in America, straight, white Christian people. This conservative conception of religious freedom is meant to uphold the dominance of people who have always chiefly held cultural and political power in this country, and equate "freedom" with the punishment of anyone who deviates from the Christian, patriarchal norms in place.

In 2018, three states—Kansas, Oklahoma, and Colorado—introduced bills that would all but ban gay couples from adopting. A few months later, the U.S. House Appropriations Committee approved an amendment to a bill that would allow religious adoption agencies to block same-sex couples on the basis of sexual orientation. The amendment was introduced by an anti-abortion lawmaker representing Alabama, which is certainly something to remember next time a self-identified pro-lifer tells women seeking abortion care to just put their baby up for adoption. Over the course of 2017, more than 129 anti-LGBTQ bills were introduced in state legislatures across the country.

Despite Trump's campaign trail promises to support LG-BTQ Americans, his presidential administration has seen us take terrifying steps backward on LGBTQ rights on the federal level, and enact policies to encourage targeted discrimination against this community. In 2017, Attorney General Jeff Sessions reversed a policy that included protections for transgender people from discrimination in Title VII of the Civil Rights Act. That same summer, President Trump announced a ban on trans people in the military that had the potential to cost the U.S. military $960 million, according to a study by the Palm Center and the Naval Postgraduate School. All this, despite using fiscal conservatism and the idea that trans people are inherent societal burdens to justify this policy of blatant intolerance.

The Trump administration's war on Planned Parenthood and sexual health education is also a direct blow to queer people, and queer young people, in particular, placing them at increased risk of contracting sexually transmitted diseases or experiencing unsafe sexual encounters. In 2015, when the state of Indiana defunded Planned Parenthood, a county that lost its only clinic experienced an HIV outbreak that involved an average of 20 new reported cases of HIV per week for 10 consecutive weeks.

In the first year of Trump's presidency, Education Secretary Betsy DeVos announced her department would no longer investigate complaints about transgender students being barred from bathrooms, arguing trans students' right to use the bathroom of their gender identity was not protected under Title IX. DeVos repeatedly declined to affirm whether the department would protect the rights of LGBTQ students against discrimination, although her 2018 proposal to give $1 billion to private schools that can legally discriminate on the basis of orientation and identity should speak volumes.

In schools across the country, LGBTQ students and trans students in particular disproportionately face school disciplinary action, such as suspension, expulsion, and even dress code violations for wearing clothing not in line with the sex they were assigned at birth. Disparate rates of punishment are even worse for queer students of color and queer students with disabilities. This ostracism and punishment of LGBTQ young people in schools has consistently yielded disproportionately high dropout rates, as well as the jarringly high rates of homelessness among this demographic.

As the "Beyond I Do" campaign highlights, 55 percent of LGBTQ people report having experienced some form of discrimination as of 2018. And while 79 percent of all American allies have said they support equal rights, 80 percent of these self-identified allies incorrectly believe that it's illegal to fire, deny service to, or evict people on the basis of orientation or gender identity. Solidarity has to entail more than espousing progressive values at a time when mainstream attitudes have shifted to the point that doing so has become convenient, even profitable. There has to be ongoing education and listening, a concerted effort to know about the real, lived experiences of people who are subjected to identity-based oppression, and see through right-wing narratives of gaslighting.

Perhaps our country is nowhere near as homophobic as it once was. But the right-wing, anti-LGBTQ faction of this country still controls far more of the messaging around the LGBTQ experience than most of us realize. The idea that queer people no longer face challenges and political disenfranchisement solely because of a few gay TV characters and politicians sprinkled here and there is right-wing fantasy. But it's a fantasy that has also infected the thinking of liberal-leaning allies, the vast majority of whom believe that the discrimination LGBTQ people face every day isn't happening, according to the aforementioned polling.

The notion that LGBTQ people no longer face oppression is a hindrance to the community's attempts to make progress that remains much-needed, a hindrance, even, to their survival.

As of 2018, the life expectancy of the average trans person stands at roughly 30 to 32 years. One in five of all transgender people in the United States are homeless or housing insecure. Some other highly telling stats: LGBTQ youth are 120 percent more likely than their straight peers to experience homelessness, and as many as 40 percent of all homeless young people are queer; 21 percent of LGBTQ people living alone in the U.S. make less than $12,000 per year.

And despite the popularity of state and local-level bans on trans people using the restroom of their gender across the country, trans people are far more likely to be assaulted than to commit assault in bathrooms. In and out of bathrooms, queer people experience sexual violence at disproportionately high rates. According to the Human Rights Campaign in 2018, 44 percent of lesbian and 61 percent of bisexual women have experienced rape, physical violence, or domestic abuse, compared to 35 percent of heterosexual women. Twenty-six percent of gay and 37 percent of bisexual men have experienced the aforementioned forms of abuse, compared to 29 percent of heterosexual men. A 2015 survey revealed 47 percent of trans people are sexually assaulted at some point in their lifetime. And these rates are substantially higher for queer people of color.

Over the course of 2017, the first year of the Trump presidency, reported homicides of queer men increased by 400 percent.

HOMOPHOBIA, TRANSPHOBIA and general intolerance for queer people didn't magically end when marriage equality became the law of the land. On the other hand, marriage equality has arguably preceded a political moment of negligent, dangerous passivity.

At the 2016 Republican National Convention, the openly gay, libertarian venture capitalist Peter Thiel took the podium to offer his endorsement of Donald Trump. In an interview with *The New York Times* a few months later, Thiel said, "For speaking at the Republican convention, I got attacked way more by liberal gay people than by conservative Christian people."

The implication of this quote seemed to be that today, people who support and espouse contrarian ideologies face more oppression and cultural ostracism than gay people do. Of course, as of 2018, Thiel's net worth stands at roughly $2.5 billion. It's safe to say he'll never be subjected to the same indignities as low-income LGBTQ people, such as being evicted or fired from work, and the myriad threats they face on a daily basis to their safety and wellness due to their identity.

And as for the social ostracism that conservative people purport to face, it's important to understand the vast difference between being stood up to or faced with the social and professional consequences of hateful, oppressive speech, and being subjected to actual oppression for one's immutable identity traits.

The suggestion that homophobes somehow today face more oppression than gay people do is a particularly hard sell, considering at the convention Thiel spoke at, Mike Pence—a man who has supported public funding for "gay conversion therapy," rejects marriage equality, and helped oversee the spread of a deathly HIV epidemic in Indiana as Governor—was anointed the Republican Party's vice presidential nominee.

Deathly intolerance remains rampant in our institutions and among our elected leaders. In recent years, particularly since *Obergefell* in 2015, the erasure of this deathly intolerance from mainstream visibility has posed a threat almost as grave. The solution to prevalent ignorance among LGBTQ allies is relatively simple: listening.

It's imperative that we help the LGBTQ community reclaim the narrative power around their experience in America. It's imperative that we see through fearmongering narratives constructed by conservative politicians, who remain so accustomed to privilege and heteronormativity that they regard the most basic representation of anyone who isn't straight as a terrifying existential threat.

And while listening is critical, no queer person owes any obligation to educate or prove their experiences with oppression to anyone. It's on allies to be real, active allies, and fight a culture of gaslighting that worsens the LGBTQ community's living standards by erasing their lived, authentic experiences. This can only be achieved through awareness, speaking out, and, perhaps most importantly, never pretending that homophobia and oppression magically vanished with marriage equality.

EQUITY, EQUALITY
AND THE POLITICS OF IDENTITY

The term "identity politics," or the acknowledgment of identity-based social difference in politics, became a runaway hit across the country—and the political spectrum—in the wake of the 2016 presidential election, mostly as a means to explain the election's shocking outcome. In the face of the greatest threat to marginalized people's rights and living standards in modern history through the election of Donald Trump, I guess the common thinking was, why not blame the Trump presidency on their existence, and the audacity of Democratic politicians to acknowledge said existence? Op-ed after op-ed by esteemed, often even liberal-leaning columnists at reputable papers like *The New York Times* or *Washington Post* certainly followed this line of thinking.

Everything except race, gender, and purportedly identity-neutral policies suddenly became "identity politics." Women's human right to access affordable, safe, legal abortion, which could determine their ability to work, go to school, provide for themselves and their families, and even survive? Identity politics. Black and brown people demanding the reform of a criminal justice system that has stripped them of dignity and economic opportunity for generations? Identity politics.

In a 2016 speech sometime after the election, Bernie Sanders criticized a woman running to be the second Latina U.S. Senator in history, saying, "It is not good enough for someone to say, 'I'm a woman! Vote for me!' No, that's not good enough. One of the struggles that you're going to be seeing in the Democratic Party is whether we go beyond identity politics."

But what does "beyond identity politics" even mean? Who wins when we choose to willfully ignore social difference, rather than acknowledge and proactively address the systemic inequities that arise from it? Who wins, and who loses?

Certainly, liberalism is imperfect. Certainly, capitalism is highly imperfect. But you'll have to excuse me if I'm skeptical of the narrative that Democratic-socialist policies and a sweeping platform of—albeit much-needed—progressive economic policies will eradicate all forms of oppression. The perspective that gender and race neutrality, if they go hand-in-hand with a progressive economic platform, would be a cure-all, one-size-fits-all solution for everyone isn't just misguided—it's also an innocuous, perhaps well-meaning form of gaslighting. It erases how economic struggles are disproportionately shouldered by people of color and women, and, unlike for white men, the struggles of marginalized people often extend beyond the economic, and take form in a wide range of potent, discriminatory forces.

In the aftermath of the 2016 election, Clinton, who won the majority of votes of low-income Americans (53 to 41 percent) and Americans who were most concerned about the economy (52 to 42 percent), was criticized for utilizing "identity politics," while Trump was praised even by his opponents for fleshing out a "unifying" message. Of course, Trump had relied heavily on identity politics—white, male rage and anxiety, specifically; we just don't call it "identity politics" because white men remain understood as the default in this country—not just by Trump supporters, but by white, male economic progressives. The mere acknowledgment of women and minorities, and how vastly our experiences differ from the default of the white man, remains universally political and controversial.

Identity-neutral rhetoric, even in the realm of progressive politics, can be actively harmful if they erase or trivialize inherent social difference.

Look, I get it: Politics is about finding as much unifying common ground as possible, and rallying as many people to your base as you can. But equality isn't achieved by pretending that all of our experiences are the same. In fact, doing so can only really have the opposite effect, as existing inequality will consequently grow as a result of this neglect.

IN MAY 2018, Illinois became the 37th state to ratify the Equal Rights Amendment, putting the United States just one state away from ratifying it into the Constitution.

The ERA was first introduced in the 1970s, the same decade that saw the U.S. legalize birth control for unmarried women and abortion on the federal level. In other words, the '70s were a decade of phenomenal progress for women's rights, which made the eventual downfall of the ERA shocking and heartbreaking. A key reason the amendment has yet to be ratified by the three-fourths majority of states necessary was the potent rhetoric of the contemporary counter-movement, led by women and men rallying under the banner of Phyllis Schlafly.

Schlafly argued that ratifying the ERA would lead to women being drafted and losing protective legislation that accorded women workers safer, often softer working conditions than those of their male counterparts. Schlafly's arguments fundamentally ignored how feminists actively oppose the draft for men and women alike and support safe and fair working conditions for people of all genders. Her movement was essentially the 1970s version of asking feminists why men can't hit women but can hit other men—a childish dig that ignores how feminists generally don't want anyone hitting anyone.

Today, the ERA remains as relevant as ever, in part because as of the summer of 2018, we're one state away from ratifying it, and ERA bills are currently floating in the legislatures of a handful of states as of publication. The modern movement for the ERA offers critical insight into the relatively new conversation around the differences between equity and equality, which belie crucial debates about gender empowerment and diversity programs, as well as affirmative action policies. The most oft-made mistake in our constructs of what constitutes equality is the belief that equality means ignoring existing difference. In light of this, the word "equity" has become more popularized among feminists and progressives, who acknowledge how sweepingly equal treatment can be harmful in neglecting to proactively take action and combat existing disparities, allowing these existing disparities to grow as a result.

In sharp contrast with Schlafly's concerns, the ERA would regard women as having equal status with men, which isn't the same as sweepingly equating men and women's very different experiences within the patriarchy and applying harmful gender-blind policies.

From the myriad legal and economic barriers to accessing reproductive health care, to an ongoing epidemic of gendered sexual violence, women's experiences remain dangerously isolated from those of most men. Thirty-four percent of the homeless population comprises families, 90 percent of which are headed by women; between 22 and 57 percent of homeless women report that they are domestic violence survivors. Across the board, gender gaps remain rampant in lucrative fields and high-paying, executive positions.

An apt example of persistent, gender-based inequality that gender-blind, sweepingly equal treatment would not remedy is the gender wage gap. The wage gap exists largely in connection with these aforementioned phenomena: gender gaps in high-paying work; gender gaps in potential role models working in lucrative fields, whom boys and girls can identify with; discrimination—conscious or unconscious—in who is more authoritative and deserving of raises and promotions; devaluation of feminized lines of work; and proven discrimination in pay negotiations and family leave policy.

Jobs and fields that become female-dominated often see decreases in pay in tandem with demographic shifts. And when it comes to highly comparable jobs that involve roughly the same work but are male-dominated, these often receive higher pay, according to a 2016 study by Cornell. Studies have shown that women in the workplace negotiate for higher pay at roughly equal rates as their male counterparts, but are 25 percent less likely to receive raises, effectively dispelling with the victim-blaming myth that women are paid less because of some intrinsic failure to take initiative. In the same vein, maternal leave policies—which often fail to include fathers, LGBTQ parents, and parents of adopted children—result in women being 8 percent less likely to receive raises and promotions. Maternal and not family leave policies reinforce the idea that all women will become mothers, and parenthood will exclusively alter women's ability to commit to their jobs, but not men's.

In other words, women continue to face ugly sexism in the workplace, which often goes beyond pay disparities to include abuses as grave as sexual harassment and exploitation, and smaller but frustrating things like everyday exclusion from "boys' club" meetings, or male employees receiving credit for the ideas of their female peers.

Eighty-one percent of women report experiencing some form of sexual harassment in the workplace, and as for the other aforementioned phenomena, there's really no way to quantify these everyday experiences. We can only tell by the stats of male CEO's and billionaires that "boys' clubs" across all industries are rampant, and are almost certainly costing women key workplace and leadership opportunities when men in positions of power fail to reach across the aisle or consider the power and necessity of diversity.

The absence of specific protections for women's rights in the workplace, such as the right to ask co-workers what their salary is without retaliation, the right to not be asked what one's previous salary was, and requirements that employers justify salary disparities between male and female employees who are doing similar work and have similar experience, has the direct effect of increasing workplace inequality by passively allowing it to continue. In recent years, we have witnessed policy decisions drag us backward on progress made in the Obama era—namely, the Trump administration's 2017 decision to end an Obama-era policy that required companies to report the salaries of their employees, which would expose gaps in pay for women employees as well as people of color.

As the wage gap currently stands, women make roughly 20 percent less than men, and that disparity only increases for black, Latinx, and Native American women. Thanks to the Trump administration's 2017 policy reversal, the absence of up-to-date statistics and transparency will also have the effect of enabling pay disparities to continue, without any means to raise awareness about the issue and demand that our lawmakers proactively enact policy change to address this.

The attitudes that drive political and cultural rejection of workplace gender protections and diversity programs are wide-ranging. At best, they emerge from the erroneous understanding that equality has already been achieved now that we no longer live in an era where women are shut out of education and the workforce, and job postings are no longer gender-segregated. At worst, they emerge from naked sexism and notions of male superiority—specifically, the idea that women's circumstances are bleaker than men's, solely because women are somehow naturally, inherently inferior.

In the summer of 2017, a then-Google employee's anti-diversity memo was widely circulated within the company, and eventually on the internet. The manifesto included such hits as, "We need to stop assuming gender gaps imply sexism," and also claimed women are underrepresented in STEM jobs and earn less than men because of natural traits that make them less intelligent and suited to the STEM field. "Differences in distributions of traits between men and women may in part explain why we don't have 50% representation of women in tech and leadership. Discrimination to reach equal representation is unfair, divisive, and bad for business," he wrote.

The employee who authored the memo was subsequently fired by Google in a laudable, perfectly legal decision by the private company. Plenty of people lose their jobs every day for far less than creating hostile work environments and perpetuating gendered animus. Imagine being a woman and having to work in the same office, even the same company, as someone who is vocal in their convictions that you are inferior and only have your job because of diversity programs. Nonetheless, unsurprisingly, Google's decision sparked fevered backlash among right-wing advocates arguing the company had violated the employee's free speech rights, that "political correctness" had once again run amuck.

Google is foremost a business—and a business running on innovation and diverse ideas. To that end, it's well within Google's best interests to create a work environment in which all employees feel comfortable and respected in sharing their ideas. And this is especially the case for employees representing groups that are traditionally excluded from positions of decision-making power in the STEM field, who are better positioned to bring new, unexplored ideas to the table. Diversity is an invaluable vehicle for creativity, and the added lens of gender within STEM and other male-dominated fields could have critical impact on their output.

That's why gender empowerment programs matter, and everyone benefits from them in some way or another. Groups that specifically train women, recruit women, and instill in women leadership and other valuable workplace skills exist to acknowledge the marginalization of women within traditionally male fields, and the workforce in general. They acknowledge that women are far less likely to find mentors in male-dominated lines of work, that young women and girls are far less likely to be actively encouraged to pursue STEM growing up, and the disparate power dynamics that inherently exist in male-dominated workspaces. They acknowledge the prevalence of sexual harassment across industries, and that women in fields led by men may be even more likely to encounter exploitation and abuse.

And yet, in 2018, women's magazines began to report on a mounting trend of men filing lawsuits against women's empowerment groups.

As of 2018, Yale University and the University of Southern California face investigations by the Department of Education for offering scholarships and other programs exclusively available to women. Organizations like Chic CEO, The Wing, and Ladies Get Paid, among other groups that provide women-exclusive social spaces and professional networking opportunities, face state investigations for violating men's civil rights. One report from 2018 detailed the antics of a man who had made hundreds of thousands of dollars through filing lawsuits against gender empowerment groups and programs.

The premise of these lawsuits is that efforts to dismantle present cross-industry male hegemony are somehow an attack on men's rights, that men's inability to access or benefit from certain programs and events—as they are able to access and benefit from just about everything else in patriarchal society—somehow erases their overall advantage. When you're accustomed to everything being about you, made for you, catered to your experience and your existence, any departure from this must feel like a radical attack on your rights—specifically, your imagined right to advantage.

A similar attitude underlies the prototypical anti-#MeToo moderates' arguments against the movement—that male artists and creators who are accused of sexual misconduct should not be denied opportunities because of these allegations. ("Let their private lives be private!").

I'm all for giving famous people and their loved ones space and privacy, and I support everyone's right to have a personal life. You'll find feminists generally are in favor of this, seeing as respecting someone's humanity means respecting their privacy.

But sexual assault and abuse are not just run-of-the-mill personal life matters; to imply that they are creates a false equivalence between, say, sexual assault and consensual extramarital affairs. (It's absolutely wild to me how much more coverage President Trump's alleged extramarital affairs with Stormy Daniels, Karen McDougal and others received, in contrast with the abysmal coverage of allegations of sexual abuse levied against him.) Failure to hold sexual predators accountable, and continuing to bestow opportunities upon them gives implicit support to this behavior, sending the message that men can treat people however they want without any professional consequences.

That said, firing people for accusations of mistreating coworkers or creating hostile work environments is hardly radical; ask anyone who works in human resources. Talent and experience mean nothing if you lack the capacity to work respectfully with other people, and certainly if you practice abusive behavior.

And to that end, the thing about men who are accused of sexual abuse, and, in particular, male artists, actors and creators, is that misogyny has a tendency to infect their art, and influence the stories they tell. Side-by-side with their published work, allegations of abuse against Woody Allen and allegations of misconduct and misogyny directed at author Junot Diaz make this all too clear.

Misconduct and sexual abuse by people in positions of power don't exclusively affect them as individuals. Their actions can hardly be confined to their "personal lives," when they affect the safety and opportunities of all women in their industry. Powerful men are often the gatekeepers of their respective fields. A man in power can end a woman's career on a whim, based on whether or not she sleeps with him or is silent about his abusiveness.

And if you really want to be angry about how unfair it is that talented people are excluded and denied opportunities from creative spaces, think about all the people who are talented but denied opportunities every day, not due to their behavior and treatment of others, but identity-based bias and discrimination, or lack of network connections due to economic marginalization—factors that, unlike practicing sexual harassment, are out of their locus of control.

Men and women lack equal opportunities, equal treatment, and equal experiences in the workplace, as well as professional and academic environments in general. To avoid continuing this inequality requires proactive policies and programs that uplift women from an inherent disadvantage. This may not be "equality," per traditional, context-neutral definitions. But the suggestion that empowerment and diversity programs are somehow unfair is pure gaslighting, and the erasure of meaningful context into the vast disparities that undercut every aspect of women's experiences in the workplace. When we do nothing about these existing inequalities, we pretend women's condition in society is their own fault, rather than the result of systemic oppression and failure to acknowledge and address this oppression.

The absence of equality isn't inherently injustice. Doggedly pursuing equality when what we really need is equity—a recognition of existing social difference and proactive work to rectify this—is often the most unfair thing we can do.

OF COURSE, ANYONE WHO IS FAMILIAR with the equity versus equality debate understands the extent to which it underlies ongoing conflict around affirmative action. White people who have been rejected by institutions of higher learning have been challenging policies that allow race to be considered in college admissions and hiring practices in general for decades. But more recently, as of 2018, Asian-American student plaintiffs have been taking center stage.

As an Asian-American woman and the daughter of immigrants, I understand the expectation that this issue would somehow be complicated or difficult for me to take a stance on. But it's not.

It's difficult to believe any of the arguments that affirmative action proponents are somehow the "racist" ones when affirmative action opponents are the ones who will pounce at any opportunity to sweepingly discredit black or brown people's achievements as the purported products of "affirmative action." It's a lazy argument, a condescending argument, a factually inaccurate argument, and above all, a racist one.

Opponents of affirmative action purport that affirmative action itself is condescending by suggesting that "lowering" standards for certain groups is insulting to them. It's crucial that we see through this patronizing rhetoric. The erasure of underprivileged minority groups' unique and challenging experiences in this country is rooted in gaslighting, the pretense that systemic oppression has magically ceased to exist, that we've all had the same opportunities in life, that none of us have faced jarring discrimination in a country built for and centered around the experiences of white people and wealthy people.

Turning a blind eye to existing inequality only exacerbates it, pretends that those who are disadvantaged are to blame for their disadvantage. And further, to object to affirmative action is also to erase how all groups—regardless of whether they are the direct beneficiaries of diversity programs—benefit substantially from cultural heterogeneity in their lives.

Despite the conflict in my community about whether we should support affirmative action—a conflict that arises from the narrative that affirmative action policies hurt Asian-American students and families—and despite how many argue that Asian-American immigrants come to the U.S. with the same poverty and hardship of other people of color who are more likely to "benefit" from affirmative action, I support it wholeheartedly.

The narrative of affirmative action as inherently harmful to Asian-American students ignores how "Asian American" encompasses a far greater variety of groups in the United States than most people are aware of, which goes back to the need for more diverse spaces, so we can all be aware of things like this. Some Asian-American groups are among the least likely demographics in the country to attend college.

Drawing from my own experiences, I come from an upper-middle-class, predominantly Asian-American community, and attended a high school rife with resentment and mockery of affirmative action. My high school was a competitive environment, and I genuinely felt for my peers and the tremendous pressure they shouldered to succeed in the traditional sense: earn perfect grades, perfect standardized testing scores, admission into a top-ranked university. I felt that pressure, too—but I also acknowledged the tremendous privilege that I was born into, the product of my immigrant parents' hard work along with other institutional factors.

My parents, like many immigrants, came to the country with nothing; they put themselves through school waiting tables and working graveyard shifts at 7-Eleven, and they saved every penny they earned so that someday, they could give me and my two sisters the highly privileged childhoods that we had.

The United States also has a history of oppressing Asian immigrants that shouldn't be glossed over. Capping immigration quotas from Asian countries, Japanese internment, discriminatory court rulings against Asian-American-owned businesses—the list goes on. But in either case, quite different from many other black and brown communities, while my parents and other Asian-American immigrants came to America with nothing, they also did not come to this country with incarcerated family, nor were they strapped by intergenerational poverty and perceptions and stereotypes of them as dangerous, violent, criminal or lazy. In contrast, research has shown how racism affects black Americans' access to housing, employment, car insurance, health care, and every aspect of their living standards, and what they are able to provide for their families.

Car insurance companies charge higher rates to people from black communities than people from white communities, regardless of how safe the black person's neighborhood is, and even if it is objectively safer than the white person's. White convicts are more likely than black people without criminal records to be hired for the same jobs. And as for black and brown youth, jarring double standards occur early: Black students are more likely to face more severe disciplinary action for the same infractions as white students, and black youth are more likely to be targeted by police. Young black men are between nine and 16 times more likely than any other group to be killed by police officers, and those who are killed are often fathers, sons, and providers to their families.

Today's black families are forced to exist in a country that remains ravaged by mass incarceration, racist policing, and continued hate crimes and white supremacist terror attacks. State-sanctioned segregation was just two short generations ago, and the generational consequences of the Jim Crow era and slavery have persisted through the years precisely due to problematic notions about what equality means, which have placed arbitrary constraints on policies meant to expand civil and human rights in the U.S. for decades.

In order to stand in solidarity with fellow people of color, it's crucial for Asian-American people to recognize how we may share many experiences with oppression and everyday racism with all minority groups, but to sweepingly conflate our experiences with those of black and brown people is to erase crucial realities that continue to divide our experiences. Affirmative action is about respect for the equal status of all people, with a cognizance of social difference, and cognizance that treating people with fundamentally different lived experiences sweepingly equally only widens existing inequalities.

Over the course of this country's modern history, we have long been on a journey—one that often ebbs and flows—to correct for the injustice and trauma upon which this nation was built, and recognize the lingering residue of these foundations. But along the way, many have internalized the idea that anything that does not directly benefit certain groups of people—in particular, those born into privilege—is inherently unfair and oppressive by nature of its partial exclusivity. And yet, this perspective plucks affirmative action's situational exclusivity out of crucial context.

Far be it from me to say that Asian-American students who protest affirmative action policies are being exploited by white leaders of the movement against affirmative action. Far be it from me to condescend to them and suggest that they don't know any better, that they don't know what's best for them. But the reality is that whether it's their intention or not, Asian Americans who collaborate with white opponents of affirmative action are actively participating in the erasure of the institution of white privilege. In refusing to acknowledge differences between our experiences as Asian Americans and those of black and brown communities, we are complicit in the gaslighting of a nation, and perpetuate the dangerous message that equality means ignoring difference.

In many ways, affirmative action in itself is—obviously—not enough. It promotes respectability politics that uplift the most "respectable" members of marginalized groups, but, as Michelle Alexander points out in *The New Jim Crow*, ignore existential issues experienced by all other members. The school-to-prison pipeline, police violence, substance abuse, and human trafficking are just a few issues that young people in communities of color disproportionately struggle with, and I daresay all of these issues pose a more severe threat than not getting into an Ivy League. And amid new revelations about how segregated many neighborhoods and schools across the country remain, the onus must be on universities to treat diversity and affirmative action programs as more than numbers, and promote inclusivity and authentic cultural interaction on campuses—anything less would fall short of affirmative action's ultimate goals of cultural education in higher learning.

Perhaps there are valid criticisms of affirmative action and its limits in promoting equity, but nothing could make the consideration of race in college or any applications a bad thing. Race, like gender, orientation, and all other identity-based facets, distinctly impacts our experiences and often our ideas and outlook on the world around us. White people and wealthy Asian people are deluding themselves if they think schooling on homogeneous campuses or working in homogeneous offices would in any way benefit them, rather than deprive them of an expanded worldview.

In the same vein, white people do not lose anything when minority groups gain rights and resources that were formerly only accessible to white people. They may lose exclusive ownership of opportunities and resources, but by no means is loss of monopoly the same as loss of opportunity.

In this country, social difference remains rampant. I don't say this because it brings me joy, or because I want inequality to exist. I say it because I know the first step to move forward and fix problems is to acknowledge that they're there.

WHO OWNS THE STREETS?

Over the course of her lifetime in public service, and particularly on the 2016 presidential campaign trail, Hillary Clinton was told to smile, well, a lot. I was never totally sure how to explain to even some of my more supportive male friends who asked why this was so offensive. In truth, if you have to ask the question at all, it's probably because you've never walked down a busy street as a woman or girl.

Hearing that command—to smile—among other forms of street harassment is pretty much an everyday experience for women and girls. Frankly, all marginalized people—people of color, LGBTQ folks, religious minorities—experience some form of street harassment regularly on the basis of their identities. Street harassment can range from your standard catcalls to stalking, and based on how you respond or don't respond, it can escalate into heavy profanity, threats, and even violence.

Even when it doesn't escalate to physical violence, public, gendered harassment can still be terrifying, especially if you're alone or riding public transportation. For me, a couple of incidents in particular come to mind. One Saturday, I was riding the LA metro reading a book when a man in his mid-to-late forties sat next to me, exchanged pleasantries, and despite receiving zero indicator that I was interested in conversation, proceeded to press me on my plans and my heritage (Where was I from? No, where was I *really* from?). When I persisted in dodging eye contact and serving minimal, transparently disinterested responses, he proceeded to lecture me, raising his voice so that everyone at least in our car could hear, about how impolite I was being, how I had failed to pick up on social cues and offer respectful, quality conversation. I apologized that he felt that way, and eventually he moved to the next car, planted himself next to another young woman, and I don't know what happened next; almost immediately after he left me, I forfeited my seat and ran to the farthest car I could get to.

Another time, on a train in the Bay Area, I was, again, sitting alone reading a book. A group of young men were jeering and making lewd comments directed at young women in the car, which predominantly comprised women and girls of all ages. When I made the mistake of looking up at them, they hurled similar comments in my direction, with the caveat of added racism. An old woman promptly came and sat next to me, perhaps seeing that I was visibly rattled. I was 19 at the time and street harassment wasn't new to me; but it felt particularly jarring when trapped on a moving vehicle, forced to sit there and take the degrading commentary without any real options to stand up for myself that wouldn't just make things worse.

In either case, to clarify for anyone who may be confused about why being told to smile is offensive, it's simple, really. The implication is that as a woman, your expression, demeanor, and general appearance are meant to cater to the male experience, to entertain and please men; that everything you do as a woman is about male comfort, male approval, male attention. And that's exactly why stringent, gendered dress codes in schools promote sexism, too. They suggest that classrooms are male spaces, that the male experience is the priority, and girls are merely visual distractions rather than equals to their male peers.

Young women are raised to regard any and all male attention as flattery and feel an obligation to reward it, or as we see in street harassment, run the risk of being called a "bitch." That's why women who reject men who go on to commit violent acts, or quite literally even kill the women who reject them, are often directly or indirectly blamed for these violent acts committed by men. Thinkpieces by male authors about men's imagined right to sexual intercourse and women's bodies often follow in the wake of incel attacks, sending a clear message: If women don't return male attention in a satisfactory manner, responsibility for what they do next is placed on our shoulders. In other words, women and girls are bound by obligation to enjoy, be grateful for, or at the very least, passively shoulder the harassment to which we're subjected without complaint.

Perhaps that's why, despite how more than 99 percent of women have reported experiencing some form of street harassment, reforms to address this and promote women's safety in public places have been abysmal: because women and girls are too often gaslit into believing that catcalls and other street harassment are flattery and flirtation, and if we feel uncomfortable with this, then that's our problem.

Street harassment and the expectation that women walk from one place to another solely for the entertainment and pleasure of men fundamentally reflect an issue of ownership—specifically, male ownership and entitlement to our bodies, as well as all public spaces.

The preeminent rationale is often that if women don't want male "flattery," the onus is on us, then, to dress differently, or not go out at night, or drive instead of walking or taking the bus, or change our walking path altogether, perhaps shell out the high costs of a cab or Lyft. But as long as we're in the sight line of men in public spaces, they can say and treat us as they please, our comfort and safety and ability to occupy space in public without being shamed and degraded, be damned.

––––––––––

OF COURSE, #METOO HAS CHANGED SOME THINGS. While reforms to address sexual abuse within the legal system have generally been abysmal, it's not insignificant that roughly 86 percent of Americans surveyed by NPR at the end of 2017 have said they support "zero tolerance" policies for sexual harassment, shortly after the inception of the #MeToo movement. Around the world, countries like France and the Philippines have even moved to criminalize street harassment by imposing fines on offenders and involving law enforcement.

In the United States, handling street harassment often falls upon cities. Most criminal codes include disturbance of the peace, stalking, assault, and similar behaviors that are often in play in street harassment, but not street harassment itself. In 2018, the District of Columbia city council passed a bill to establish a formal, inclusive and intersectional definition of street harassment, in addition to public education programs to prevent street harassment, rather than criminalize street harassment and obligate women of marginalized identities who may fear or distrust law enforcement to interact with police officers. Additionally, criminalization of street harassment could also have the effect of targeting homeless people, if begging—an act that is often requisite to homeless people's survival—is regarded as street harassment.

The aforementioned, tangible actions being taken to help make women safer in public spaces are a direct product of shifting cultural perceptions of sexual harassment in the wake of #MeToo. Cultural movements are powerful and have the ability to produce real, meaningful change.

In 2016, Shannon Coulter launched the #GrabYourWallet movement, calling on those who reject the politics and ideologies of the Trump administration to boycott the Trump family's products—Ivanka's fashion line, Donald Trump's hotels and resorts, et cetera—and call on stores that carry their products to drop them. Within months, Nordstrom, Neiman Marcus, and other popular shopping platforms dropped Ivanka's collection. In 2018, Santa Clara County voters voted to recall County Judge Aaron Persky, the judge who sentenced Brock Turner to just six months in jail for rape, after a far-reaching, two-year, grassroots campaign led by Stanford Professor Michelle Dauber, reflecting the #MeToo movement's capacity to yield tangible, lasting change within the judicial system.

Cultural attitudes and social pressure matter. They're the difference between passively allowing public spaces to be toxic, uncomfortable and dangerous environments for women and girls, and galvanizing communities to take action and ensure women's safety in public.

Street harassment is the perfect example of how everyday sexism infects literally every aspect of women's lives. Surely there are men—men of color, trans men, and others from marginalized backgrounds—whose experiences with public harassment have also instilled in them a fear of public spaces. I can't speak for them, but speaking for myself, if I had a dollar for every time I decisively changed my walking route to a more long-winded one, or drove, or grudgingly shelled out the money for a Lyft to avoid walking down a path where I know I'll experience harassment—well, I would be able to afford all the Lyfts.

Street harassment and all of the everyday ways women are forced to reshape our lives to work around it cost us time and money. Sexism costs us time and money.

It all adds up and is often cumulatively devastating. And if not devastating, then at the very least, what we face is a nuisance, and an unnecessary, unfair, gendered nuisance, at that. That's what I mean when I say street harassment is about ownership—the idea that men own the streets, and therefore, when women walk on these streets, we do so as pieces of meat for male objectification. But street harassment is about more, even, than objectification. It's also fundamentally about ownership of privilege, about ownership of society—who belongs here, in public, and who doesn't.

SO, THE WAR ON WOMEN IS HAPPENING.
WHAT DO WE DO?

"Pro-life" women frustrate me. People of all genders who disdain talking "politics"—or, you know, acknowledging the existence of pressing, existential human rights issues we should all care about—frustrate me. But there's something I want to make clear: It's no woman or any marginalized person's obligation to fix society's most urgent, oppressive problems any more than it is the obligation of people of privilege.

It shouldn't be on women's shoulders to fix misogyny, when we certainly didn't create it. Just as I'm annoyed by anyone who chooses to not be a feminist, of course I'm annoyed by women who aren't feminists. But once again, the obligation to be a feminist or an activist shouldn't exist solely for women. Certainly, as women, all of us are beneficiaries of the feminist movement and its progress and myriad victories over time. That's indisputable. But women of generations past fought and died for our right to choose to be active players in our destinies, or, conversely, choose to be complicit in advancing and enabling patriarchal institutions, just as so many men choose to be every day.

By no means am I defending complicity—I find it universally frustrating, and certainly believe in the moral obligation to take civic action to promote social justice. But women should have the right to do anything and everything that men have the right to.

The War on Women—a political and cultural agenda of controlling, punishing, dismissing, and gaslighting women—exists, and it was not created by women. We are not responsible for it, and yet we are on the frontlines of the war, leading the resistance.

And there's plenty of reasons for why that is. For starters, the premise that reproductive rights, sexual violence, and the wage gap are "women's issues" is dangerously isolating. Women comprise a growing majority of the population, are increasingly phasing out men as household breadwinners, and every single person across the board regardless of gender is affected by whether people are able to control our bodies and achieve economic security. The only reason women's experiences are relegated to the soft, oft-dismissed fringe of "women's issues" is that men and the male experience are still universally recognized as the default identity in this country.

I don't mean to say the term "women's issues" shouldn't exist—our experiences are often different from men's due to misogyny and patriarchy, and I'm all for acknowledging rather than erasing these existing disparities. What needs to change is our lack of respect for women's issues, and the pressure that is placed on women to draw male approval to validate the issues that disproportionately affect us.

Think of well-meaning and certainly important movements like Emma Watson's #HeForShe, or the pro-choice movement's Men for Choice. Solidarity and allyship will always be important. People with privilege should always be encouraged to utilize that privilege to support and uplift those who lack it. But I can't help but resent that we don't live in a world where women can say, "This is what's happening to us, believe us and take us seriously," without having to speak through male mouthpieces.

TO ALL THE MEN OUT THERE who want to be better allies, first, remember and never forget this: We don't need your approval. We don't need your validation.

In your everyday conversations with women about literally anything, try listening and gauging whether the woman you're speaking with really needs or even wants you to explain something to her. Ask questions and actively listen before inserting your own opinions. Try letting her lead the conversation. Don't interrupt, and respond to and acknowledge what's said to you before shifting the subject of a conversation.

Lastly and very importantly, if you encounter news about something that you understand to be a "women's issue," don't reflexively ignore it.

It doesn't matter how many female friends you have, or how much you love your mother and your sisters and your daughters and your nieces, or how many women you hire, and so on, and so forth. Women aren't tokens, and you shouldn't need to collect relationships with us to see women as human beings. Sure, be motivated to speak up for and be an ally to the amazing women in your life—but don't do it just for them. Do it for all of us. Do it because we deserve human rights—all of us, not just any one, specific woman in your life.

We need everyone in this fight. Because contrary to the beliefs espoused by every right-wing narrative, every Twitter troll, every contrarian in our econ classes and every man who will never cede an opportunity to show up and speak over us, the War on Women is happening. And men have a moral obligation to participate in this fight and work to rectify this system of inequality that we, women, certainly did not create.

THERE'S ONLY ONE WAY FOR WOMEN to win the war on our rights and bodies: by showing up. By having faith and certainty in our experiences and our understandings of our experiences, no matter how many men and internet trolls try to discredit and gaslight us. That said, it's entirely natural to experience self-doubt, and that's where supporting other women comes in.

As women, we share myriad universal experiences with everyday sexism, and when men show up at our doorstep, on our social media posts, and everywhere, frankly, with gas lamps in hand to tell us "Well, actually," we have to show up for each other, affirm each other, support each other, refuse to be silent.

We stand hand-in-hand, arm-in-arm in our experiences with being talked over, in having our narratives and recollections of our own experiences erased and condescended to. Where others don't care, where others don't believe—we have to be there and show up every day for the women in our lives, caring and believing our hearts out.

Call your representatives daily (yes, it matters), show up to rallies in your community, share educational social justice content on social media, and in any way you can, proactively support the women and girls in your life. Supporting women is without a doubt an inherently political act.

If you're a woman and you find yourself apologizing, or qualifying your arguments with "I think," or "that's just my opinion," all the time, certainly don't feel guilty. The internalized misogyny we all struggle with isn't our fault—and it's time for us to stop feeling bad about things that aren't our fault.

Lastly, don't allow anyone to convince you that you care too much, or that you care disproportionately about something that isn't important. The most potent tool at the War on Women's disposal is gaslighting, making women feel crazy for caring and having the audacity to believe that we deserve rights, we deserve more, and we shouldn't be made to settle. They think that if they tell us to "prove it" enough times, we'll stop believing in the reality of our own experiences, and subsequently, stop fighting.

So, let me be clear. At the end of the day, the best approach to gauging whether something "really" matters is as simple as this: If you care, then it matters. Full stop. No further explanation necessary.

KYLIE CHEUNG is a feminist writer and activist. Her writing about women's rights, reproductive justice, and national politics has been published in *Salon, AlterNet, Rewire, DAME Magazine, Brit + Co, Teen Vogue*, and others. In her spare time, Kylie enjoys reading political memoirs, volunteering for political campaigns, and re-watching *The Office*. Follow her on Twitter @kylietcheung, and learn more about her writing at www.kyliecheung.tumblr.com.

THOUGHT CATALOG
CATALOG
Books

THOUGHT CATALOG BOOKS is a publishing house owned by The Thought & Expression Company, an independent media group founded in 2010 and based in Brooklyn, NY. Committed to facilitating thought and expression in order to engender a more attentive, imaginative, and exciting world, we aim to help people become better listeners and communicators.

Powered by Collective World, we're a community of creative people across the globe. Visit us on the web at thoughtcatalog. com or explore more of our books at shopcatalog.com. If you'd like to join our community, apply at www.collective.world.

Made in the USA
San Bernardino, CA
26 November 2018